P R A I S E   F O R

THE EXECUTIVE LEAP

"The Executive Leap *provides savvy advice for executives considering a career move. It brings into sharp focus the level of detail and preparation that are required for an executive to successfully reengineer his or her career.*"

—STACEY O'BRYAN

CEO, Quick Weight Loss Centers

"*This is an excellent reference guide with proven best practices for executives to find and land the role they want. The Executive* Leap *reflects insights from a world-class executive recruiter that have proven effective time and again. I highly recommend this book for those searching for a role as well as hiring managers.*"

—DIRK MONTGOMERY

CFO and EVP of global supply chain, Hooters International

"After reading The Executive Leap *twice, I urge everyone in an executive capacity or otherwise looking to gain an edge in his or her job search to get this book and gain the knowledge and advice Mike's extensive executive search experience highlights. I have worked with Mike personally and have experienced his strategic advice in action and up close. His strategies work. Mike works!"*

—PATRICK D.

SVP Procurement, Fortune 100 Healthcare Company

THE

EXECUTIVE LEAP

THE
EXECUTIVE
LEAP

BREAKTHROUGH STRATEGIES TO LAND
YOUR NEXT TOP JOB

MIKE SUDERMANN

Published by Advantage, Charleston, South Carolina.
Member of Advantage Media Group.

ADVANTAGE is a registered trademark, and the Advantage colophon is a trademark of Advantage Media Group, Inc.

Printed in the United States of America.

10 9 8 7 6 5 4 3 2 1

ISBN: 978-1-59932-756-3
LCCN: 2017931707

Cover design by Katie Biondo.

This publication is designed to provide accurate and authoritative information in regard to the subject matter covered. It is sold with the understanding that the publisher is not engaged in rendering legal, accounting, or other professional services. If legal advice or other expert assistance is required, the services of a competent professional person should be sought.

Advantage Media Group is proud to be a part of the Tree Neutral® program. Tree Neutral offsets the number of trees consumed in the production and printing of this book by taking proactive steps such as planting trees in direct proportion to the number of trees used to print books. To learn more about Tree Neutral, please visit **www.treeneutral.com.**

Advantage Media Group is a publisher of business, self-improvement, and professional development books. We help entrepreneurs, business leaders, and professionals share their Stories, Passion, and Knowledge to help others Learn & Grow. Do you have a manuscript or book idea that you would like us to consider for publishing? Please visit **advantagefamily.com** or call **1.866.775.1696.**

To my dad, Fred Sudermann, the world's greatest relationship builder who taught me to always do what is right, not what is easy.

To my wife, Emily, who has always been supportive throughout my executive-search career. She has been there through the highs and lows, and she and our kids, Jackson and Whitley, have endured my working vacations. I love each of you with all my heart.

DISCLAIMER

Names and other identifying details in the experiences Mike describes have been altered to maintain client confidentiality.

TABLE OF CONTENTS

ACKNOWLEDGMENTS

I'd like to thank all the executives I have worked with over the years. You trusted me to help you revamp your resume, discreetly market you, champion you into a client, advise you on interview strategies, provide counsel regarding job opportunities, offer negotiations, and more. Without your trust in working with me, none of the experiences shared in this book would have been realized.

I would like to specifically thank Michele Williams and Mitch Miles for sharing ideas and providing support in this endeavor. Lastly, thanks to my team at Advantage Media for their help in making this book a reality.

ABOUT THE AUTHOR

In April 2006, Mike Sudermann received a call from a friend who had recently joined a boutique executive-search firm. His friend was adamant that Mike would make an excellent executive-search consultant and he should speak to the CEO about joining the firm.

Up to that point, Mike had spent the first seventeen years after graduating college working successfully in clinical education, banking, and entrepreneurial endeavors.

Looking for a career leap, Mike agreed to talk to the CEO, who hired him on the spot, with one caveat—he would have to make a placement within ninety days. Although never one to back down from a challenge, Mike was hesitant. After all, he would have to quit his current job and move to a new role in a new industry. After considerable reflection and a blessing from his wife, Mike accepted and entered the recruiting business.

Later Mike would learn the ninety-day time frame—the firm's standard litmus test for "newbies"—had been achieved by only a handful of people in the firm's twenty-year history. Undaunted, Mike met the challenge and within five years had created a formidable retained-search practice, placing executives in roles throughout the US. He had built a reputation as more than just a recruiter or headhunter: he had become an executive strategic-search advisor.

As an executive strategic-search advisor, Mike wears several hats at once. He's a trusted partner to his clients looking to hire top-grade executive talent and the job search expert that leaders turn to for advice on career moves, job offers, resumes, severance packages, compensation-package negotiations, interview strategies, relocation tips, and more.

From 2006 to 2011, Mike built his reputation on the increasingly in-demand industry of executive recruiting. During that time, Mike reviewed an estimated fifty thousand resumes, talked to over fourteen thousand hiring managers, and guided over five hundred executives in career-endeavor strategies.

In 2011, Mike started his own firm, Ascent Select Talent Capital—now called Ascent Select. Within weeks of setting up shop, Ascent Select was hired by a multibillion-dollar international apparel distributor for a large recruiting project—forty-five placements in eight weeks, nearly one placement per day. Fellow executive recruiters thought he was crazy to take on the contract, especially considering the time frame was originally twelve weeks which in itself was very aggressive and such a short length that even a "big city" search firm had first turned down the project. Within eight weeks, Mike had completed his placements and was asked by the client to take over the project management responsibilities of the other contract recruiters to fill the remaining operations roles. Within six months, he had made over seventy placements.

The project grew to more than 160 placements in three years and included roles such as vice presidents of human resources, finance, tax, controller, technology, and treasurer; numerous directors and managers; and other team members. To achieve these numbers, Mike talked to more than three thousand candidates. Ultimately, Mike and Ascent Select built the IT, finance, operations, human resources, and customer-service departments for the apparel distributor. At the same time, he continued building strategic partnerships with other clients and made numerous placements throughout the United States.

Mike and Ascent Select have built a reputation for providing top-caliber talent quickly without sacrificing quality. To date, Mike has personally reviewed over eighty thousand resumes, worked with over one thousand executives, and made more than three hundred placements.

With a 2015 CEO search for a $200 million apparel company in Sydney, Australia, Ascent Select forged its first international partnership. Today, the award-winning firm has handpicked nine affiliated search partners to work directly with his firm, alongside another one hundred-plus affiliate partners located in the US and around the world.

Recognized globally as a top-twenty search firm by NPA Worldwide, Ascent Select is hired for its expertise in placement of executives around the world; the company can present top talent in as little as seven business days, enabling clients to make hiring decisions in near real-time and fill roles in weeks instead of months. Mike works with clients on direct-hire placements, project-based recruiting, outplacement, and global employment outsourcing (GEO).

MAKING THE EXECUTIVE LEAP

What is *the executive leap*?

Whether you're in the corner office at the top of the company building or still climbing the corporate ladder on the verge of a breakthrough to the top, the leap from your current job to a new executive role is one of the most daunting challenges you'll ever face.

A leap is a more than a big jump—when you leap, part of you understands that you don't quite know exactly where you'll land. That means a leap is often an act of blind faith.

But why would you ever leap on blind faith alone? As the age-old saying goes: "Look before you leap."

This book is your opportunity to look—to learn my proven set of breakthrough strategies and land your next top job.

In today's world, the Internet and the automated hiring process have blown the rungs off the old executive-career ladder. The ladder is a relic of the past, from a predigital time when it wasn't so crowded at the top, when you could make a few calls on Monday, have a few lunches midweek, and land the executive role of your dreams over drinks on Friday.

I wrote *The Executive Leap* to help you break through the complexities of today's challenging job-search market. Today, 51 percent of *satisfied* workers are open to new job opportunities.[1] Add in those that have been downsized and you quickly become just another face in the crowd. Not only is the executive market plentiful, but it's only a few clicks away for hiring managers and executive recruiters. If you don't look before you leap, you risk being passed by the competition—that is, unless you have an executive-level strategy to land your next executive role.

> If you don't look before you leap, you risk being passed by the competition—that is, unless you have an executive-level strategy to land your next executive role.

More important than your competition is your compensation. According to Forbes, when changing jobs, the average increase in compensation nationally is 15 percent. Executives who follow my proven strategies are typically seeing upwards of 30–40 percent and sometimes as much as a 59 percent increase in compensation. Why settle for 15 percent when you could double or even triple that national average?[2]

As a successful professional, you build and use strategies daily to successfully navigate business and maximize results. Making a job

---

1   Jobvite, *Job Seeker Nation Study 2016: Where Job Seekers Stand on the Economy, Job Security, and the Future of Work*, 4.

2   Cameron Keng, "Employees Who Stay In Companies Longer Than Two Years Get Paid 50% Less," *Forbes*, June 22, 2014, http://www.forbes.com/sites/cameronkeng/2014/06/22/employees-that-stay-in-companies-longer-than-2-years-get-paid-50-less/#63d3e434210e.

transition is no different. Try to land your next top job—and top compensation—without following a set of strategies and you risk failure. Reminds me of that quote from Ben Franklin, "If you fail to plan, you are planning to fail."

When looking for a new job, professionals seek the following:

- compensation: 52 percent for millenials; 70 percent for established professionals aged 40–54
- location / geography: 50 percent
- growth opportunities 43 percent
- health benefits: 43 percent
- work-life balance: 33 percent
- flexibility / virtual working from home: 23 percent; 31 percent for millenials[3]

THE EXECUTIVE LEAP'S BREAKTHROUGH STRATEGIES

Over the past decade working with executives, I have personally reviewed over eighty thousand resumes, talked with tens of thousands of hiring managers, negotiated hundreds of compensations packages, made hundreds of placements, and have led thousands of executives through strategies for landing a new role. In that time, I can say that the executive job market has changed dramatically. It's no wonder so many executives out there get frustrated when looking to land a new role.

---

3   Jobvite, *Job Seeker Nation Study 2016: Where Job Seekers Stand on the Economy, Job Security, and the Future of Work*, 8.

The majority of the executives I speak with on a daily basis are overwhelmed by the prospect or are underinformed of the process of making the leap. They wonder why it takes so long to land a great job, with great pay, that meets their specific requirements. Many professionals think dusting off the resume, adding a few bullet points, and applying for a position posted online or contacting a few friends is all they need to do. Those measures, once the norm in the 1990s, are no longer enough, by any stretch of the imagination.

If you're used to networking with friends or calling in a favor, you'll be in for a big surprise.

What are executives looking to land a new role supposed to do?

To answer your questions in the simplest way possible, I wrote this book. In these pages, I've collected my thousands of hours of executive-advising experience, analysis, and best practical tips into a set of breakthrough strategies. Each point in the executive-leap process—from rebuilding your resume to accepting a job offer with top compensation better than the national average—is broken down into strategies, one strategy per chapter. Whether you need a resume that sings, a LinkedIn-profile makeover, or detailed practical instructions on the entire interview process, you'll find the strategy here to help you make the leap.

BREAKTHROUGH TIP: Hiring managers today are using social media platforms to search for candidates, review candidate accomplishments, and advertise job opportunities. Chapters 4 and 5 detail how to make the most of your online activities.

If you're like many other executives, maybe it's been a few years since you were last in the job market for a new executive role. Perhaps you don't even realize that you're behind the times or need help until you're six months into the process and haven't landed a top job, so let me share one scenario that demonstrates why you need this book's breakthrough strategies to succeed in today's hiring climate.

PHILLIP'S STORY

Recently, Phillip, a CEO who had been in his current role for twenty-plus years, began looking to make a career change. In his previous role he had "hung the moon." The notes on him were: "highly regarded, maintains an extensive network, exceptional executive leader and visionary, and brings substantial value that can be leveraged by a new employer." Sound familiar?

To Phillip's surprise, he struggled to land a new role quickly.

Eventually, he realized that making calls to old friends was not enough to land a top job or top compensation in today's market. When he and I first spoke, we talked at length about his career goals, next role, industry, locations, and more. I advised him to update his approach. He willingly agreed, knowing that technology had changed everything about his business over the past decade, so of course he should expect the executive job-search process to have changed, too.

As his strategic-search advisor, I walked him through my breakthrough strategies, which include a standout resume rebuilt for the digital age, an advanced LinkedIn profile, surefire answers to trick-or-trap interview questions, and other pre- and post-interview essentials to break through.

Once he managed to get up to speed with the change, we implemented his new plan of attack on all fronts.

Soon he was interviewing for leading CEO roles, ultimately landing a position that gave him a new CEO role in his industry, a 30 percent increase in compensation, and a phenomenal benefits package. Without the breakthrough strategies, he would have struggled to make the executive leap, likely settling for a less-than role or less-than compensation.

THE #1 REASON YOU SHOULD READ THIS BOOK

"Great," you say. "Mike, you're the expert in executive search, placement, resumes, interviews, and online strategies, and you helped some yahoo get a job. Big deal. What else can you do for me?"

My reply? The breakthrough strategies in this book will show you how to land your next top job *and* **earn an increase in executive-level compensation at or above the national average of 15 percent.**

KEN'S STORY

A vice president of finance from a major beverage producer called me requesting a tiebreaker between him and his wife on whether or not he should take what appeared to be a very lucrative regional CFO job offer. While a fantastic opportunity, the couple was struggling with a decision. After talking with the executive and discussing the pros and cons of the position, he took my advice and declined the offer. Two months later the beverage producer reached out again—this time, the company had sweetened the deal. He called me again to discuss, and I advised him to take the job—which he did.

Ken's sweetened deal meant an increase in compensation of 40 percent. Today, after several additional moves, he's the national CFO of that major beverage organization.

But that's not the end of the story.

Over the years, I've advised Ken about everything from job-search strategy, career transitions, and talent acquisition. I'm able to provide this kind of strategic advice to executives because I have assisted hundreds of executives on complex job offers, salaries, benefits, stock options, relocation packages, etc. As a result, I know what salaries and bonuses should be for specific roles: manager, director, vice president, senior vice president, and C-suite. I know exactly what salaries should be in different parts of the country; for instance, the salary in San Francisco may be similar to New York but substantially different than in Kansas City. I understand the impact of state taxes, or lack thereof, on salary, for a relocating executive—whether in the US or elsewhere in the world.

In short, I know how to create a variety of compensation packages for specific individuals. Today, that means more than just base and bonus. It means relocation bonus, sign-on, car allowance, stock options, equity, healthcare, noncompete, severance, gas cards, wellness memberships, and a variety of other add-ons.

CONTENTS OF THE BOOK

The Executive Leap's breakthrough strategies show how to make the leap that positions you as the top candidate and earns you the best possible compensation.

In the chapter's ahead, I'll take you step-by-step through every strategy needed to help you "look before you leap." Chapter 1 reviews today's job search and the value of having someone fighting for you in your corner—I call that someone a strategic-search advisor (which is an executive recruiter and advisor merged into one). Chapter 2 guides you through all you need to know to rewrite your resume, including resume myths, the concept of "city-bus marketing," and details on how to rebuild your resume in thirds. Chapter 3 explains the cover-letter strategy, with samples that show you exactly what to do (and not do).

After we've covered the traditional basics, chapter 4 discusses social media and the importance of expanding your digital footprint to ensure that people know about your industry niche beyond your resume. Chapter 5 shines light on your LinkedIn profile, the must-do social site for business professionals. (Don't even *think* about skipping the chapter on LinkedIn, as you'll need every strategy presented to land your next top role and top compensation!)

Chapter 6 discusses interview strategies: what to do before and during the interview to ensure that you maximize your competitive advantage and leap the competition. Chapter 7 gives you some trick-or-trap questions (and winning answers) to circumvent any interview obstacle. Chapter 8 walks you through the entire interview conversation. To wrap things up, chapter 9 covers what to do after the interview is complete. By the time we get to the book's conclusion, you'll have an excellent understanding of what to do to make the executive leap.

C H A P T E R   1

TODAY'S JOB MARKET AND THE STRATEGIC-SEARCH ADVISOR

Whenever I speak with professionals looking to make an executive leap, I first remind them: "The executive job search world has changed dramatically over the past decade. If you're applying for an executive role using the same strategies that you used in 2006 or—look out—1996, then there's a high probability you'll struggle to land a new role in a timely manner in today's market."

For many, hearing that landing a top job requires new strategies is a much-needed wake-up call. Before we dive into the latest strategic advice, here's another: Are you willing to settle? Are you willing to lose to the competition and miss out on top jobs and top compensation?

If you're willing to settle, then you can put the book down now. You can't make the executive leap if you're willing to settle.

What are the signs that you're settling? Sending out resumes but getting little to no response; interviewing but never landing; receiving compensation-increase offers *at or below* the national average of 15 percent—each tells me that you're not correctly positioning yourself to make the leap. Each tells me that you're behind the times or need some serious strategic advice.

If everything has changed over the past decade, then what's the executive job-search and hiring landscape today? In other words: How do you position yourself to leap the competition?

THE TWENTY-FIRST CENTURY EXECUTIVE JOB SEARCH

As a successful business leader, you stay current with trends in your industry. You adapt with the regular changes in technology. Your executive job search requires the same approach.

Gone are the days when you sent your resume via e-mail or snail mail to a newspaper or job-board posting. Gone are the hiring managers who have all the time in the world to review resumes. Hiring managers today are often overloaded with multiple tasks, meetings, and massive time constraints. As a result, they have very little time to review a resume—today you're lucky if you get ten seconds.

In the past, a company would get your resume; and if luck would have it, you were invited for an interview; and if you were a good fit, you were hired. Nowadays, once a company gets your resume, they are already checking out your LinkedIn profile, Facebook, and other sites to make sure you are who you say you are—are you a thought leader in your industry niche? Does your profile suggest you'd fit in with the company culture?

Differentiating yourself twenty or even ten years ago was predominantly done on your resume. In today's talent market, you have to be savvy and have a strategy that includes not only your resume but also social media such as LinkedIn and a well-refined interview approach. *This is the bare minimum.*

Executive recruiters and hiring managers are experts at both judging a book by its cover and reading between the lines. For example: Resume fonts and formatting have changed over the years. By your resume alone, I can tell your approximate age, your energy level, and how successful your job search is going to be. By your cover letter, which speaks volumes about you in a positive or negative way, I can read how much you want the job and whether or not you'd be the right fit. One look at your LinkedIn profile tells me a great deal about your endeavor to be successful in your search for a new role. Finally, by the way you answer (and ask!) interview questions, I can tell if you're a small fish in a big pond or a shark that doesn't sleep.

You are judged by every last detail in the hiring process. Does that unsettle you? Be unsettled then, because the last thing you want is to do is "wing it" or approach the process the same way you did when you were saving your resume on a floppy disk.

Most executives learn the hard way that the job search has changed. The good news? Those executives behind the times are your competition. Apply my breakthrough strategies and you're already miles ahead.

THE VALUE OF BREAKTHROUGH STRATEGIES

At some point early on, soon after your decision to make the executive leap, did you do a Google search? Did you Google: "How to write a resume?" or "How to write an executive resume?" What about: "How to create an executive-level LinkedIn page?" or "How to prepare for an executive interview?"

Your Google searches likely resulted in hundreds of articles, some recent but many out of date, that promised you tips, traps, and "the top-ten tricks to consider." While some of the advice may be current or helpful, let me tell you, what you need is a one-stop shop for every breakthrough strategy—current and *proven a thousand times over*—from the leading expert in the executive job-search field.

An article from a Google search can tell you how to craft a professional LinkedIn page—but it can't tell you how to make a LinkedIn page that will *wow* recruiters and hiring managers enough to garner you a guaranteed call from an executive recruiter or hiring manager.

As you've pondered the executive leap, you've likely spoken to someone outside of your family about what the leap entails. Did you ask a mentor or a colleague for advice and practical tips? Getting knowledge wherever you can is all well and good, but advice that works for one person doesn't always apply to another.

When reading all the articles and books you could find and speaking to all the mentors and colleagues in your network, did anyone ever mention how to receive a compensation increase of more than the 15 percent national average? That should be one of many strategic questions.

The difference between an online article or a mentor and this book is that my advice is based on the experiences of *hundreds of executive searches over the past decade*. Nowhere else—not on Google, not in your Rolodex, nowhere—will you find all the strategies collected together to teach you how to land your next top job. This book is your best companion for making the executive leap.

But what about a compensation increase *greater* than the 15 percent national average, you ask? Thankfully, you don't need to go it alone to find the answer.

Now that you know the rules of the executive job-search game have changed and you're committed to reading *The Executive Leap*, you have two options:

1. You can apply my breakthrough strategies on your own.

2. Or you can work with a strategic-search advisor.

If you're an executive who wants a top job *and* top compensation, you may need more than a companion book. *You need a strategic-search advisor in your corner.*

THE STRATEGIC-SEARCH ADVISOR

I'm an executive recruiter—that's my unofficial job title. My official job title: strategic-search advisor. In other words, an executive **strategic-search advisor** is two roles combined into one:

1. **Executive Recruiter.** Companies hire me to identify, source, and recruit professionals that reside in the top 10 percent in their industry and functional niche and present them for specific roles. I recruit the cream of the crop.

2. **Advisor.** I counsel professionals, teaching them my proven strategies for making the executive leap. Together, we practice, practice, practice. As a result, they learn how to position themselves to leap to the next level in their career and compensation.

Of the many benefits to having a Strategic Search Advisor help you make the executive leap, one of the biggest is that I can help you see the forest through the trees. By that I mean you likely have a lot of information from colleagues, books, Google searches, and your own experience. My strategies will allow you to clearly decide how to *best* execute a leap.

As your strategic-search advisor, I understand the executive marketplace. I know the salary ranges for specific roles, what the opportunities are for your industry or functional niche, approximately how long it will take you to land, and where you stand compared to your competition. In addition, I provide certainty on every part of the hiring process: from what to use on your resume to how to prepare for the trap questions in the interviews.

What sets a strategic-search advisor above the rest?

Your colleague's advice on how he or she made the executive leap is an opinion. My breakthrough strategies on how to make the executive leap are fact—field-tested and proven after hundreds of thousands of hours.

To show you what I mean, here's a real-life, strategic-search advisor story.

ANDREW'S STORY

A few months ago, a company retained my firm for a CFO search. After talking with more than a hundred professionals in three weeks, my team presented the top four candidates to the company. Each candidate could have done the job equally well. To decide their favorite, the company defaulted to the usual method: ranking the candidates by evaluating their resumes. Andrew ranked fourth. The company CEO thought Andrew's resume was poorly written and wasn't sold on him being worth the time to bring in for an interview. Fortunately, as the candidate's champion, I was able to convince the CEO to look past the resume and interview the candidate.

Prior to their interviews, I offered all four candidates my tailored strategic-interview session. I worked with the top-ranked candidate for only five minutes because he had limited time to talk. The number-two ranked candidate passed on the guidance because he said he was "good to go." Number three told me in our phone conversation that he was listening but not in a position to take notes and did not have any questions for me during the call. Andrew asked a lot of questions, said he took several pages of notes, and called me the next day to review a few things prior to the interview.

Upon completing the interviews with the first three candidates, the client thought they were ready to make an offer, but because they had already scheduled Andrew, they honored the interview commitment. I'll give you one guess what happened next. Andrew knocked the socks off the CEO during his interview.

Immediately after the interview, a company representative called to tell me they wanted to hire Andrew and asked me to make him an offer before his departing flight home. Not only did he get the offer, but he received a whopping 59 percent increase in base salary and more than 100 percent increase in total compensation!

Bottom Line: I give strategic advice. I counsel you through your search endeavor, helping you make decisions that are appropriate for you and your family. If a job is wrong for you, I advise you against it. I won't shoehorn somebody into a role. If you're an ideal fit, I will advocate on your behalf.

TAKE MY ADVICE

By the time you finish this book, you will have the know-how to build a high-performance resume that compels any reader to call you for an interview. You will have keen insight on navigating social media and LinkedIn to your advantage and differentiate you from the competition. You will be equipped with the life-changing interview and post-interview strategies to ultimately land your next top job and best-possible compensation.

I developed my breakthrough strategies having worked with thousands of executives over the last decade and spending countless hours researching to stay attuned to industry statistics, trends, and resources. As a result of my studies, experiences, and candid client feedback, I have developed proven strategies for helping executives position themselves to land their next top job.

The key to success is in your hands; these breakthrough strategies are proven and work wonders if you use them. Take my advice, don't settle, and you will succeed.

C H A P T E R   2

RESUMES

Test your resume knowledge. Circle *True* or *False*.

1. Someone will read your resume front to back, no matter what.

    True   *False*

2. The best font to use on a resume is Times New Roman.

    True   *False*

3. An objective or a summary is essential on a resume.

    True   *False*

4. Graphics and color should always be used on resume.

    True   *False*

5. White space on a resume is a waste of space.

    True   *False*

When making the executive leap, your resume is the first step in *making* or *breaking* your candidacy for landing a new role. Why is the resume so important?

When changing jobs, you *know* you are a superstar. But does your resume *show* it? Based on how you answered the true-or-false questions to open this chapter, your resume may show that you're unaware of how resume design can affect your search endeavor. The resume has changed over the years, and yours is most likely out of date or needs fine-tuning. Either way, it's not doing you any favors.

I appreciate the confidence in anyone who does a job well and identifies with that role, but to those who think they're already number one, I say: "Prove it to me. Because based on your resume and the other several hundred people I've talked to this week, I'm not seeing it." That's essentially what I tell executives who ask me what the competition is like, and I continue with this reminder: "However good you think you are for this role, your competition is probably better." Hiring managers and executive recruiters typically start the vetting process with your resume, so it should scream, "I'm exactly what you're looking for. Call me now!"

 **BREAKTHROUGH TIP:** Your resume is a marketing document used solely to secure an interview.

In the pages ahead, I'll expose old resume truths you thought still held water as myths you need to drain from your mind. What you need to learn is this: The resume represents *you*. It tells me about you and what you bring to an organization. It speaks for you when you are not present. If you answered *false* to most of the quiz questions, your resume may be in good shape, or it might need some tweaking. Either way, by the end of this chapter you'll know exactly how to rewrite your resume using my breakthrough strategies—city-bus marketing, the rule of thirds, core competencies, keywords, and more—to help land your next top job.

To show you what I mean, let's begin with a story.

JOHN'S STORY

John was a former vice president of communications who had been recently downsized. He had an extensive advertising and marketing background and years and years of experience, but he was not seeing any results from his job-search endeavors. After he was introduced to me, we completely retooled his resume to include some attention-grabbers. We reformatted his resume with emphasis on the rule of thirds, core competencies, key accomplishments, and specific keywords—all of which I'll discuss later in this chapter.

In short, we turned his resume into a marketing document.

Working with John, it struck me that here was someone who was in marketing—he was an executive who understood print as a media. He knew how to communicate a message, to make an impact for the organizations he worked with, but he couldn't do it for himself.

Within the first week after he sent out his retooled resume, he was getting calls for interviews. Within about two weeks of working with me, he was interviewing. In less than a month, he had offers for several excellent positions.

In the end, he landed a new position with a $35,000 increase in salary and a 45 percent overall increase in total compensation, without having to relocate.

While John had a champion in his corner, not everyone has a strategic-search advisor to reposition his or her resume. How do you make the executive leap even without a strategic-search advisor on your side? How do you convey to companies, hiring managers, and executive recruiters you are the best? How do you leap the competition?

To help you better understand the enormous value the resume brings to the table, let me share with you *The Executive Leap*'s **top-seven resume myths**.

Resume Myth #1: Someone will read your resume front to back, no matter what

BREAKTHROUGH TIP: Your resume must stand out in a crowded market. For every hundred resumes an executive recruiter or company hiring manager wades through, fifty will be from professional painters, car salesmen, chefs, or bar owners who always wanted to be a chief financial officer!

Imagine for a minute you are the hiring manager. You are up to your eyeballs in work, meetings, conference calls, and a multitude of other seemingly more important things to do than sift through stacks of resumes to identify the best-possible candidate to interview. You need hours to go through the pile but don't have even five minutes to commit to the task. So how are you going to tackle the first step in your search process? Instead of reading each resume one by one, you are going to glance at them—or worse, have human resources or internal recruiters review them. Due to your time constraints, in a matter of seconds you and your team are going to look for knock-out-factors, not buy-in factors.

When you consider that this scenario is what's happening to resumes you've sent to a recruiter, submitted online, mailed in, or even delivered in person, then you know why yours must be designed to convey to the reviewer that you are indeed a superstar, someone with relevant experience, who's worth having a conversation with. Your resume should subliminally say to the reviewer, *Go ahead, keep reading the entire resume, you won't be sorry. I will bring you value, save you money, improve processes, and give you a great return on investment. Bring me in for an interview!*

Your resume is the door opener, and if it is not designed correctly, most of the doors you encounter will stay closed.

Unfortunately, in most cases, your resume will not be read front to back. That's why it must have what I call "**city-bus marketing**" recall. What do I mean? Before city buses became rolling murals with splashy graphics covering them front to back, they were rolling advertise-ments with framed billboards mounted on their exteriors below the passenger windows. Those billboards advertised things like a floral-delivery company or local dentistry. Imagine yourself in a big city, circa 1980, and a bus goes by at ten or fifteen mph. On the side of the bus is a billboard with something that catches your eye; with just a quick glance, you're able to gather enough information for you to remember: 1-800-SERVICE. You remember the number on the bus

> *Your resume is the door opener, and if it is not designed correctly, most of the doors you encounter will stay closed.*

because it's clearly spelled out and it's something that *answers a need you have*. You don't remember the company name, or the graphics, or anything else. You do, however, remember that snippet of information (in this case, the phone number) because it's going to fill a need you have—in this case, service for something.

So how does that relate to your resume? Like the advertisement on the side of the city bus, your resume is going to get a seconds-long glance. In that time, your resume must create interest, speak to a need, capture the attention of the reader, and compel him or her to take action.

> According to the executive career website TheLadders, you only have six seconds to get a recruiter's attention. A study conducted by the organization found that recruiters, human resources, and hiring managers make the "fit/ no fit decision" in about six seconds.[4] What does this mean for you? Your resume must appear professional, be formatted to clearly articulate the value you bring, and be clear and concise. It means your resume must, in that excruciatingly brief period of time, present *you* in such a way that compels the reviewer to set up an interview with you as soon as possible.

THE RULE OF THIRDS

When creating your resume for the greatest impact, it must incorporate city-bus marketing by following *the rule of thirds*. Since hiring

---

4   Will Evans, "You have 6 seconds to make an impression: How recruiters see your resume," *TheLadders*, March 21, 2012, http://info.theladders.com/inside-theladders/you-only-get-6-seconds-of-fame-make-it-count.

managers are typically looking at a large stack of resumes, yours must tell them what they need to know in the first third of the space on the page.

To create that impact visually, print out your resume on a regular 8.5-by-11-inch sheet of paper and fold it in thirds. The information on the first third of the page should include your name, address, telephone number, e-mail, and LinkedIn URL.

The remaining space on the first third should contain your *core competencies*. Those are a critical component of the first third and will usually make or break you. (I'll talk more about these in a minute.)

BREAKTHROUGH TIP: On your resume, use your cellphone number, not your home phone number. Recruiters and hiring managers are busy and don't want to leave a message for you on a home phone and wait for you to call back. The great executive-search consultants will call you at work, but I know plenty of recruiters who will dump your resume into "File 13" (a.k.a. the trash) if they cannot reach you by cell. Using a home phone number sends the message that you're not accessible and that you may not be serious about making a job change. If you want to be accessible, use your cell number. As for your e-mail address, be sure it befits the role you're applying for. No "cutesy" e-mail addresses, such as *#1pokerplayerinvegas@yahoo.com*—unless you *are* the number-one poker player in Vegas and you're applying to the Bellagio as a pit boss!

The top third of the page is all the space you're going to have to get the reviewer's attention; that's all anyone is going to digest in six seconds.

Resume Myth #2: Summaries and objectives are essential

Summaries and objectives are things of the past. They do not provide information about you fast enough for the person taking a six-second glance at your resume. The challenge is that once you've included your name, address, telephone number, LinkedIn URL, and a properly spaced summary or objective in your resume, the first third of the page is full. How many recruiters or hiring managers will actually read that block of text? Speaking from experience: not many.

Summaries were created years ago to give a reviewer of a resume a detailed portrait of the professional you, a setup that worked when people had more time on their hands. Usually the summary was between five and ten lines of copy that provided the resume reviewer a snapshot of your career: how many years of industry experience you have, management or leadership roles, particular experiences, and so on.

The same with objectives. Those were added years ago to declare to the reviewer a specific role you wanted; under a heading "Objectives," you'd list the position or role you were looking to land. The challenge with an objective is that it pigeonholes you into a particular role, and it doesn't really add value to your resume. In my decade of experience working with executives it has been rare to see an executive resume with an objective. Summaries and objectives fill critical space in the top third of your resume, which you could put to far more effective use.

Instead of a summary or objective, the top third of the page should include the heading "**Core Competencies**," followed by a bulleted list of critical words or statements that might normally be in a summary. This is easier for busy recruiters and hiring managers to read and will more quickly convey the value you can bring to an organization. Such a bulleted list *highlighting you* is an effective way to design your resume—a.k.a. marketing document—to get you an interview.

Use a simple, round bullet or square symbol. The bullets should be appropriately spaced so that they are readable on the page. And remember to take advantage of white space—use it to make your resume more readable and add to its visual appeal.

Regardless of what you do for a living, core competencies should include the industry you specialize in, your function, and keywords and key phrases (see Appendix page 157). Look to include action-able keywords, phrases, and accomplishments such as "built high-per-formance teams," "collaborative leadership," "process improvement," etc. Want to test your resume results? Set a timer for six seconds and then start reading from the top toward the first crease. How far did you get? If you're too wordy, trust me, most people won't get halfway through the first third in that six-second time frame. Make sure you include concrete numbers in your first third such as a percentage or whole number.

SAMPLE RESUME: FIRST THIRD
WITH CORE COMPETENCIES

Before:

JOHN SAMPLE

1100 Sample Aveneu, Powell, UT 43065 ■ jsample@gmail.com ■ Mobile XXX-XXXX

EXECUTIVE SUMMARY

Procurement, strategic sourcing and supply chain leader with an excellent track record of results in the CPG, food and beverage sectors. A creative thinker, effectively interacting cross-functionally and leading all procurement transformational activities to drive sustainable performance. Excellent communication and interpersonal skills. A motivated leader who leads by example through a positive attitude, integrity, proactivity, high energy level and a strong sense of urgency. Highly skilled in procurement and global strategic sourcing strategy and process development/implementation (Category Management, Strategic Sourcing, E-Procurement, etc.). World class negotiation skills within multiple levels of complexity. Excellent leadership and mentorship background, with strong experience in implementing procurement metrics/analytics, aligning business goals and objectives, embedding consistent procurement performance into various cultures, building world class procurement teams, domestic and international supplier development/management, commodity risk management, delivering significant YOY cost savings to the business and optimizing the value that Procurement brings through centralization and spend optimization. Direct, indirect, capital, contract manufacturing, benefits, IT and other areas of significant spend ownership (domestic and international).

After:

John T. Sample

1100 Sample Avenue, Powell, UT 43065 • Mobile 614-XXX-XXXX • jsample@gmail.com

CORE COMPETENCIES

Global Strategic Sourcing Leader • $800 M Spend • CPG, Food & Beverage
Collaborative • Build World-Class Procurement Teams
Commodity Risk Management • Spend Optimization • Results Driven
High Energy • Sense of Urgency • Cross Functional Leadership
Averaged $28.5 M Savings Annually

Resume Myth #3: Fonts are no big deal

Can you believe that your executive leap might never get off the ground because of a *font*? Fonts can make or break you. Take care in selecting your font. Keep in mind it needs to be easily read, elegant, clean, and professional—but not too basic. According to a recent article in the Huffington Post, the five best fonts are Calibri, Helvetica, Georgia, Ariel, and Garamond.[5] As far as size goes: Nothing so small the hiring manager needs a magnifying glass to read it—an 11- or 12-point font is ideal.

BREAKTHROUGH TIP: Times New Roman is out. Times New Roman conveys to the reviewer that you are lazy and didn't put much thought into your resume typeface. Today, there are better, more current options available. In fact, Microsoft Office 2007 replaced the program's Times New Roman standard with Calibri.

WITH THE DIGITAL RESUME, SIMPLER IS BETTER

Posting your resume on a job board such as Monster.com or Career-Builder is not typically how a senior executive lands a new role. There are, however, very well-paying roles for directors and vice president-level positions being posted online. In today's digital world, only those resumes designed and formatted with the digital upload in mind will be found. Fancy resumes that have graphics, unusual bullets, or

---

5   Andrew Lord, "The 5 Best Fonts to Use On Your Resume," *The Huffington Post*, June 12, 2015, http://www.huffingtonpost.com/2015/06/12/fonts-to-use-on-resume_n_7562714.html.

Excel charts won't download properly, certainly won't get read front to back, and likely won't be read at all. You will be invisible, while competitors whose resumes are properly formatted will be read.

Here's an example of what I mean. An executive with a very well-known US organization sent me her resume for a position my firm was filling for a client. If she had sent the resume directly to the company through its online posting, it would never have made it through the system into an interviewer's hands. Why? It was so poorly formatted the system would have kicked it out; it contained dozens of different font styles, symbols, graphs, and a variety of other components that made it difficult for software systems to read. All those extras would have translated digitally into a jumbled-up mess.

Resume reviewers who receive documents digitally want easy-to-read documents. Attractive resumes with all kinds of formatting are fine for e-mailing in a PDF format or printing and presenting to an interviewer in person. However, a digital resume uploaded when applying online requires a simpler style and setup.

Resume Myth #4: Everything must be included

 **BREAKTHROUGH TIP:** *Less is more.* Your resume should not be a data dump of your entire career.

Too much information eliminates the element of curiosity that makes a reviewer want to learn more about how you achieved such wonderful results in a particular role. The old saying, "less is more" is true on a resume. However, on the flip side, don't leave questionable gaps in your resume. Include enough information in your resume to compel the reviewer to discover how you made a positive impact for your current and/or past employers.

THE RESUME BODY: KEY ACCOMPLISHMENTS

Following your contact information and core competencies, the remaining two thirds of your resume should include your key accomplishments for each role that you've held. These can be in separate bullets or in the body of the resume—your choice of format, but again, use readable font size and spacing.

Your key accomplishments *ideally must include these three points:* how much money you've saved an organization, how much money you've made for an organization, and processes you've improved.

List your accomplishments in bullet format, ideally beginning with a number. Here is a before-and-after example of how to describe the savings your employer experienced as a result of your efforts:

Before: Worked with XYZ department to facilitate a learning, training, and development program. Saved 15 percent in costs associated with this program.

After: 15 percent saved annually with the implementation of a strategic-training development program.

This is a basic example, but it's critical in that the second bullet has the accomplishment starting with a number. People read left to right in the US, so make sure the reader understands immediately the quantifiable result first and a short description second.

NAME EXAMPLE, MBA, CPSM

Address, City, ST 112233
nameexamplemba@wsu.edu | 316-XXX-XXXX | linkedin.com/in/nameexamplemba

---

HIGH PERFORMING EXECUTIVE IN SUPPLY CHAIN, OPERATIONS, & STRATEGIC PROCUREMENT

Respected for creating influential and collaborative relationships with leaders across all business functions
Catalyst for meaningful change to achieve extraordinary business performance and financial results

Sixteen years experience building and leading supply chain transformative initiatives and build teams in high growth organizations, including process improvement, strategy, project management, and operations

CORE COMPETENCIES

Strategic Sourcing ★ Contract Negotiations ★ Vendor & Client Relationships
Long-Range Strategic Planning ★ Operational Efficiencies ★ Profitability Optimization
Lean Six Sigma Black Belt ★ Continuous Improvement ★ Data Analysis
Cost Reduction & Avoidance ★ Spend Analysis

$165 M in SAVED in past 7 years through strategic spend and contract management

---

PROFESSIONAL EXPERIENCE

COMPANY NAME   Somewhere, CA   2010 – Present
Growth during tenure: +$2.5B revenue, +123% cash, +192% net income, 346 to 950+ specialty retail stores

Director of Corporate Strategy   *(2014 – Present)*
Promoted to develop and implement Company Name long-term strategic plan in partnership with CEO, CFO, top management team. Direct process improvement, ensure innovation, and deploy strategic initiatives.

Specific Key Accomplishments:
- **Supply Chain Transformation:** key partner involved in all supply chain systems & eCommerce projects
- **Enterprise Project Management:** appointed to develop and lead new company-wide EPMO capabilities
- **Process Improvement Committee:** co-chair of cross-functional team to increase company efficiencies
- **Omni-Channel Definition and Deployment:** created strategies, and execution plans
- **Mergers and Acquisitions:** evaluated, executed, and integrated business development activities

Director of Procurement   *(2010 – 2014)*
Recruited and hired to build company's first centralized procurement organization to manage sourcing, contracting, negotiations, and vendors for $600M spend across 100% of indirect goods and services (supply chain, IT, eCommerce, marketing, real estate, finance, corporate operations, facilities, travel, HR, construction, legal, MRO). Highly involved in re-engineering inbound/outbound product logistics (TL, LTL, small parcel), acquired new technologies: Neloane, CRM, Omniture, Oracle, SAP, Manhattan, JDA, Fortna, TMS, Axcion, ADP Rackspace, ExactTarger and others.

Specific Key Accomplishments:
- **$75 M Caputured in contract savings**
- **2.6% Reduction in SG&A in first 2 years,** from 24.6% to only 22.0% of sales
- **Partnered with all SVPs** to support market evaluation, supplier sourcing, vendor selection, negotiations, contracting, and supplier relationship management. Played key strategic role in rebuilding eCommerce foundational systems, including expanding mobile and eCommerce capabilities and reach.

NAME EXAMPLE, MBA, CPSM

COMPANY NAME   The City, WY   2005 – 2010

Director of Procurement Services   *(2007 – 2010)*
Created strategic sourcing team of 25 responsible for $600M indirect spend across all global company categories for multiple eCommerce businesses, 1,000 stores, 9 distribution centers, and HQ. Implemented TMC and OBT. Administered $80 M utilities budget while evaluating hedging opportunities to drive cost reduction.

Specific Key Accomplishments
- **43% Increase ($115M) in operating cash flow** and **39% increase ($0.68) in earnings per share**
- **$70 M Savings delivered by re-negotiating contracts**
- **28X ROI** on training costs by developing and implementing high-level company wide negotiations training.
- Introduced **reverse auction bidding** to accelerate cost reduction.

Divisional Replenishment Manager   *(2005 – 2007)*
Hired to restructure a 20-person supply chain team to achieve all-time KPI highs for $1.8B of annual global inventory. Managed JIT assortment demand flow, planning and allocation strategies, purchasing, supplier management, and inventory analysis.

Specific Key Accomplishments:
- **35% Reduction in supplier lead time**
- **26% Improvement of order on-time rate and 9% Increase in fill rate.**
- **$22 M Savings** through implementation of a cross functional efficiency system

COMPANY NAME   Land of OZ, KS   2004 – 2005

Vice President of Operations
Recruited and hired to manage 70 corporate, field, and store employees at multi-channel (store, online, wholesale) start-up retailer. Led all store operations, customer service, HR, visual merchandising, eCommerce, supply chain fulfillment, post-purchase communications, and procurement during rapid growth to 15 stores in 5 states in just 2 years.

Key Accomplishments:
- **20% Reduction in turnover**
- **28% Savings in supply chain** and improved lead-time by 3-days.
- **$61 M Savings** by initiating performance evaluation criteria to improve operational efficiencies

PREVIOUS PROFESSIONAL EXPERIENCE: Inventory Planning & Management | International Service

MACY'S: Led $75M inventory allocation, planning, and distribution for high-growth 900-store fashion retailer. ANNA'S LINENS: Allocated $35M of inventory across 5,000 stores worldwide. Increased inventory turnover 8%.

EDUCATION & PROFESSIONAL TRAINING
MBA – Kansas University – Strategy and Leadership – Cum Laude – 3.762 GPA – May 2014
BA – Wichita State University – English (major), Management (minor) – 3.874 GPA – April 2001
Six Sigma Black Belt and **Lean Six Sigma**, Duke University
CPSM – Certified Professional in Supply Management, Institute for Supply Management
The Strategic Negotiator and **The Complete Skilled Negotiator**, The Gap Partnership
Strategic Procurement, Wharton School of Business

BREAKTHROUGH TIP: Do not go into detail. Create curiosity.

As we discussed earlier, too much information can be deadly. It's imperative to create curiosity so the reader has to interview you to learn how you were able to accomplish such great results. Admittedly, it can sometimes be difficult to be grammatically correct when starting with a number, but remember hiring managers want people who can achieve a return on investment. They're going to see the number and in which area of operations it was achieved—that information is what will impress the reviewer. Past success almost always determines future success and gives the organization an indication that they can expect the same or better.

SCOTT'S STORY

A chief financial officer named Scott sought me out after he missed the final cut on a new role. Despite terrific qualifications, he was simply not offered the position. In his disappointment, he decided his resume was part of the problem, so he paid a person claiming to be a "professional resume writer" $1,200 to rewrite it for him.

When Scott sent the new resume to me for my thoughts on the rewrite, I was stunned by how much his resume had changed—and not in a good way. It had gone from three pages to four. I printed the first page and folded it into thirds, set my timer to six seconds, and glanced. At the end of six seconds, I knew nothing about him. His new resume was now worse!

Scott's resume went from good to bad with the addition of more information. Basically, the rewrite removed any curiosity and thus eliminated any reason to interview him. This is a concept that people miss all the time.

What was so disappointing is that Scott's resume had good bones; all it needed was a little tweaking, not a major revamp. Afterward, it didn't have any pop; it was boring, and all the essential details were buried in four pages of long paragraphs.

While the "professional resume writer" had an English degree and was a weekly contributor to a newspaper, they had never been an executive recruiter, had no idea what hiring managers are looking for in an executive's resume, and had no experience with regard to the client's industry or functional niche. The final product, in addition to being lengthy, lacked key accomplishments and had inadequate keywords that were not related to the executive's industry expertise and functional niche. Scott set his CFO leap back and will find it challenging to land a new role simply because his resume reads like a short novel. If you were a hiring manager, would you wade through that?

Resume Myth #5: Your resume should fit on one page

Most executives have a decades-long career history, so don't try to cram twenty years of experience onto a single sheet of paper. If you have more than ten years of experience, it's highly unlikely you'll be able to fit everything onto one page. Don't be overly concerned about extending your information onto at least a second page, or possibly a third. Whatever you do, avoid using a tiny font in an effort to make your resume fit to a presumed maximum length.

Several years ago I received a resume from an executive who had over twenty years' experience crammed onto one page. The font was so small that even with bifocals I could barely read it!

For the most part, your resume should be less than four pages, unless you've written a dozen publications, been a presenter, won a number of awards, and have a patent or two. In any case, information such as this should be listed on the last page of a resume.

If your resume looks too wordy (no white space), too long, poorly formatted, or contains information not relevant to the job, it will not be read in its entirety and you will most likely not be contacted for an interview. Plain and simple.

Resume Myth #6: Keywords can be made up

Quick question: Can keywords, sometimes referred to as buzzwords, be any word you think best describes you? No. Keywords are nouns, verbs, acronyms, and key phrases about your experiences as they pertain to a particular role, functional niche, or your career experiences, and are used to attract what your audience is looking for.

For instance, let's say an organization is hiring for a senior vice president of global supply chain. Keywords that should be included range from "global supply chain" to "$3B spend" or "cost-benefit analysis." Poor keywords will handicap your resume from being noticed and can slow your endeavor to land a new top job.

BREAKTHROUGH TIP: Keywords are as important to use in your resume as they are in social media profiles, follow-up letters, cover letters, and any other written form of communication that you want or expect a prospective employer or recruiter to see. Keywords likewise play a big role in the social media realm and should be used when building your LinkedIn profile or posting on Twitter.

Although most executive-level roles are not advertised online, social media nonetheless plays a big role in identifying suitable candidates, and you will be remiss if you don't include appropriate keywords on all your brand-identity / marketing endeavors.

©Glasbergen
glasbergen.com

"You've described yourself as a 'free thinker'.
That's good because we can't afford to pay you."

KEVIN'S STORY

"That role fits me like a glove," Kevin said, in our first conversation. He was interviewing and not landing. "I can't believe they're not calling me," he went on.

I asked him if he had the specific experience the role called for, and he confirmed that he did. "Then why isn't it on your resume?" I asked, to which he replied, "Because then my resume would be four pages long."

As it turned out, his resume had way too much information in it and was getting held up in company systems or just not passing the rule of thirds test.

Once we rebuilt his resume to include appropriate keywords among a few other changes, he landed a position shortly after we started working together.

BREAKTHROUGH TIP: Avoid keywords that are adjectives. For example, "visionary" is overused and over the top; quite frankly, it's a word that someone else uses to describe you in the third person. Sprinkle keywords and phrases throughout your resume, making sure they pertain to your *functional niche*.

Resume Myth #7: Graphics, photos, and colorful text make your resume stand out

While it is tempting to use graphics, photos, and colorful text in an effort to make your resume stand out—don't do it. If you apply online to a job, your resume will load improperly and graphics will not be picked up. Or worse, your resume will not load at all. You may think you submitted your resume, but in reality it never made it into the system.

Skip the headshot. Instead, make sure it's on your LinkedIn profile. Colors and graphics should only be used on resumes you are going to send by snail mail or hand to someone in an interview. If you use color, use it in moderation and avoid pastels.

RESUME TYPES

There are basically two types of resumes: chronological and functional.

Chronological is the most-common format, in which your most-recent employment is listed first. When listing chronologically, ideally you should list both the month and the year of your employment.

Chronological resumes work particularly well for people with a stable work history—ones who don't have multiple gaps in employment. They also work well if you've been in the same role for a number of years but have changed industries. In addition, chronological resumes list titles that show your increasing levels of responsibility.

EXAMPLE SAMPLE
Address, City, ST, 11223 • examplesample@city.rr.com • Mobile 612-XXX-XXXX

CORE COMPETENCIES

Procurement Strategist • 22-Years Expertise • Indirect Procurement
Collaborative Leadership • Lean Six Sigma • Spend Analysis • Profitability Improvement
Contract Life Cycle Management • Performance Optimization • Consensus Building & Teaming
Best Practices & Benchmarking

KEY ACCOMPLISHMENTS

• Transformed XXXXXX global procurement culture by implementing key strategies
• $35 M Annual Savings at Company by creating and implementing long-term procurement strategy
• Pioneered & implemented Best-in-Class sourcing solutions

PROFESSIONAL EXPERIENCE

XXXXXXXX Inc., Wichita, KS   **12 / 2001 to Present**

Sr. Director, Indirect Procurement & Global Travel Manager   **7 / 2013 - Current**

Hired to oversee all of Indirect Procurement with a spend of $1.5 B. Responsible for creating and implementing procurement strategy for all indirect goods and services.

Key Accomplishments:
- $45 M in annual savings by redefining Company Health's indirect procurement strategy
- 50% Reduction in sourcing project cycles by developing and implementing an e-Sourcing solution.
- 40% Reduction in travel costs
- 30% Increase in compliance and transparency by creating and implementing a CAH Storefront
- Decreased contract review process while reducing legal labor expense and overall financial risk
- Created Enterprise Service and implemented across 66 Countries in EMEA, APAC & LATAM
- Established best practices in Contract Management, e-Sourcing, Spend Analytics and Dynamic Discounting.

Director Indirect Procurement   **7 / 2006 – 7 / 2013**

Promoted to implement and support best in class sourcing capabilities for all of XXXXXX global sourcing functions to include pharmaceutical and medical direct commodities, contract management, e-sourcing, spend analytics and supplier diversity.

Key Accomplishments:
- Created Center of Excellence organization and drove global adoption of core sourcing solutions
- Implemented end to end, fully automated customer contract solution to support Retail Independent business and their 3,000 customers.
- Developed Global spend analytic solution that aggregated 28 global AP systems as well as created a Travel/Expense management analytic solution that provided transparency resulting in the development of a business case to create a Global Enterprise Services.

EXAMPLE SAMPLE

Address, City, ST, 11223 • examplesample@city.rr.com • Mobile 612-XXX-XXXX

Key Accomplishments Continued ...

- Increased # of contracts created by 150% through the development of Contract Management Office that consisted of on-shore and off-shore resources shifting low value tasks from higher cost legal resources.

Manager Indirect Procurement   6 / 2005 – 7 / 2006

Promoted into this role to define and implement a supplier relationship management solution to improve and exceed IT, Legal, procurement and strategic sourcing goals.

Key Accomplishment:

- Exceeded sourcing goals
- Created and implemented strategic sourcing program saving $100 M Annual on a $2.7 B spend

Project Manager, Application Development   12 / 2001 – 6 / 2005

Key Accomplishments:

- 4% Increase in application availability from 95% to 99% within first 12-months
- Implemented electronic invoice presentation and payment solution
- Leader in formalizing and implementing XXXXXXXX Software Development Life Cycle methodology.

EDUCATION & CERTIFICATIONS

Duke University, Durham, NC   2000
Masters in Business Administration

UNC-Chapel Hill, Chapel Hill, NC   1996
Bachelor Degree in Economics

Project Management Institute
Project Management Professional Certification (PMP)

Functional resumes or *bios* focus more on skills and achievements and will oftentimes have a short summary at the top with work history at the bottom of the document. They are used for networking purposes, when you have gaps in your work history, or when past positions aren't relevant to your current career or to your future career goals. These bios can be formatted in a way that highlights your accomplishments, including specific skills, experience, and work history.

BREAKTHROUGH TIP: In lieu of a full multipage resume, the bio is always one page and is a great document to send via e-mail or snail mail to your network (friends, neighbors, previous associates, etc.) along with a note asking them to share with anyone they know who might be looking for top talent.

EMILY SAMPLE

Address, City, State
Cell Phone:
Email: name@gmail.com

GENERAL COUNSEL / VP CLAIMS / ICA President
INSURANCE / FINANCIAL SERVICES EXECUTIVE

Highly accomplished financial services / insurance executive with strategic litigation management and business operations experience. Exceptionally skilled in building teams, diplomatic negotiations, achieving results, managing multiple projects, critical thinking skills, and leadership.

- President of International Claims Association (ICA)
- $297 M in savings through life insurance claims litigation management with a 94.2% success rate
- 69.4% Reduction in Turnaround Time
- 42 % Reduction in Claims Costs

Key Skills: Litigation Management, Highly Skilled Negotiator, Developing, and Implementing Long-Term Operations Strategies, Results-driven executive who can multi-task with a passion for leading people and building high performance teams.

Juris Doctor, The Catholic University, Columbus Law School
Bachelor of Arts, Political Science, Davidson College

SELECTED ACCOMPLISHMENTS

$297 M SAVED by leading successful life insurance claim litigation throughout the United States. Hired and managed outside counsel to assist in handling caseload. Successful formulation and management of litigation strategies for all cases consistent with business goals, expectations, and budgets.

42% Cost Reduction in claims processing and 69.4% Reduction in Turnaround Time. Asked by COO to utilize expertise in long-term strategy formulation and critical analysis skills to improve claims processing efficiencies. Assumed management of a team of 60+, built new SOPs, implemented training in multiple locations and achieved corporate goals.

President of International Claims Association (ICA). After 16-years involvement in ICA and holding numerous roles within organization was elected President. Created and implemented updated online educational courses resulting in a 37% increase in online course enrollment. Initiated membership growth and retention strategy increasing membership by 17% and first year ever in history of organization did not lose a single member during my tenure. Established new digitization and automation educational content at meetings to help our members understand the impact of digital and automation is having on their businesses.

CAREER HISTORY

VP General Counsel, Company, 2015 to present. Utilizing litigation management expertise coupled with business operations and claims process improvement launch insurance digitization project across entire organization.

AVP, Life Claims & Customer Solutions, Company One, 2012 to 2015. Requested by COO to come over to business side and help improve efficiencies of claims processing, turn around and cost reductions. Successfully built high performance teams in three locations and achieved substantial improvement efficiencies.

Associate Counsel, 1996 to 2012. Hired as Associate Counsel to manage employment, fixed annuity, group and individual life and health insurance litigation nationwide on both state and federal courts. Counseled corporate business units daily on broad range of legal issues including insurance law, contract administration, employment, debt collection, and fraud. Consult state and federal regulatory issues that govern hiring prospective insurance agents and employees, underwriting new business and state insurance replacement guidelines. Drafted agents' contracts for use by over 30,000 producers representing multiple distribution channels, reviewed agency office leases and drafted third party administrative agreements

xxx-xxx-xxxx | name01@gmail.com

First M. Name
Supply Chain Executive
Spend Optimization + Strategic Sourcing + Transformation + Sustainable Savings + Procurement Operations

Expertise	**Executive Summary**

Expertise

Multi-Channel Procurement

Global Sourcing

Value Creation

Process Improvements

Turnarounds

Multi-Million Dollar Budgets

Multi-Million Dollar Negotiations

Procure to Pay

Continuous Improvement

Operations Efficiency

Spend Optimization

Executive Summary

CAREER BRAND -Supply chain transformer who drives earnings and enterprise value while streamlining operations to strengthen nimbleness and scalability. Known for turning around procurement operations and catalyzing next-level purchasing performance.

PEDIGREE -Certified Purchasing Manager with a BS in Accounting from the University of Baltimore. Possess deep purchasing experience spanning the hospitality and healthcare sectors, including co-founding a $1B group purchasing organization (GPO).

Global Sourcing ♦ Operations ♦ Procurement ♦ Supply Chain

MULTI-CHANNEL HOSPITALITY & HEALTHCARE:
- Deep supply chain transformation and operations orchestrating turnaround of $1.2 B / 700 location organization within three years and paved way for an IPO.
- Led implementation of a new strategic sourcing initiative including supply chain standardization, tactical buying, rebranding, and distributor KPI's.
- Participated in Kaizen and / lean operations strategy to ensure efficiency in operations, minimize SKUs and reduce inventory levels to eliminate waste.

PROCUREMENT TRANSFORMATION:
- Overhauled out-of-date supplier portfolio and purchasing function to save $29 M during real estate market collapse.
- Developed new supplier standardization sourcing processes saving $5 M first year.
- Heightened procurement efficiencies, developed cost savings initiatives and contract compliance metrics delivering over $45 M in direct cost savings over a 2-year period.

GLOBAL STRATEGIC SOURCING & INTERNATIONAL OPERATIONS MANAGEMENT:
- Established and rebuilt Asia sourcing office operations in Shanghai China to enable direct supply chain relationships with local manufacturers and suppliers based in AP region. Reduced supplier lead-time by 40%.
- Re-organized, managed and coached a team of 22 procurement professionals located in Europe, NA, LATAM and Asia regions into category focused and high performing global strategic sourcing team saving $10 M annually.

Professional Development

MBA – Loyola Marymount University
BS – Chemical Engineering, University of Minnesota

TRAINING & PROFESSIONAL DEVELOPMENT
Six Sigma – Black Belt Certified ♦ Certified Professional in Supply Management (CPSM)
Certification Programs in Kanban, Lean, Supplier Innovation, SAP and Others
United States Marine Corps Officer Candidate School (OCS)

AWARDS & ACHIEVEMENTS
Johnson & Johnson Standard Leadership Awards -06', 07' and 08
Johnson & Johnson Consumer Procurement Excellence Award -07'

REFERENCES

References are not typically seen on resumes anymore. Executive recruiters, hiring managers, and anyone else reviewing a resume knows that if references are needed they can be provided. Extra space (without cramming anything in) should be filled with a list of your certifications, publications, skills, or awards.

CALL IN THE PROFESSIONALS

Needless to say, avoid glaring errors in your resume! Write the document and give it to three or four people in the family or a neighbor to read over. Use spell check, then review the document carefully for spelling and punctuation errors. Print it out and read it one more time, carefully, line by line.

Regardless of whether or not you think your resume is up to par, have an executive recruiter such as myself review your resume prior to embarking on your search. Recently I had an executive reach out to me to review his resume, and I ended up championing him into one of my senior-level roles. He interviewed and made it to the final round—all because he wanted me to review his resume prior to starting his job search.

Bottom line: Regardless of whether your resume is championed into the hands of a hiring manager by a strategic-search advisor or you're pursuing a role on your own, your resume needs every advantage possible to be read in its entirety (not just given a six-second glance). It must have core competencies, bulleted accomplishments, strong keywords, enough white space, current fonts, and error-free and appropriate formatting. Meet all these criteria, and you will successfully navigate through the first step of the search process, securing interviews on your way to making the executive leap.

CHAPTER 2 READER TAKEAWAYS: RESUMES

- A resume is your brand; it represents you and speaks for you when you are not present.

- The resume is simply a marketing document designed to get you an interview.

- Follow the rule of thirds when designing your resume.

- Six seconds goes fast, so design your resume to compel your audience to read it from top to bottom.

- Summaries are old school and waste valuable marketing space.

- Paragraphs of information are important but must be strategically placed.

- Do not write an objective unless you want to be pigeonholed into a specific role.

- Be current with your font selection and don't use Times New Roman.

- Keywords and keyword phrases are an essential part of your resume; choose them wisely.

SCHEDULE YOUR *FREE* TEN-MINUTE RESUME CONSULTATION CALL WITH MIKE AT 1-844-789-LEAP

C H A P T E R   3

COVER LETTERS

Test your cover-letter knowledge. Circle *Yes* or *No*.

1. Cover letters can be as long as you want them to be.

    Yes   *No*

2. It's best to talk about what is in your resume on a cover letter.

    Yes   *No*

3. Cover letters are oftentimes considered a writing sample.

    Yes   *No*

4. Keywords or key phrases should be used in cover letters.

    Yes   *No*

5. You should always indicate why you want to work at the company.

    Yes   *No*

Has the cover letter become obsolete? Some people think so. However, they certainly help make deciding on a prospective candidate faster and oftentimes can make up for a really lousy resume. In fact, according to a survey conducted by Robert Half, 91 percent of executives polled said that a cover letter is an important part of their evaluation process.[6] A well-written cover letter will be read in its entirety as opposed to the six seconds given to a resume.

Cover letters are tailored to the opportunity and will speak directly to the reviewer regarding the expertise you bring to the position, why you want to work there, and what you know about the company and its industry. Because they are considered to be a writing sample, cover letters help executive recruiters and companies weed out candidates. A well-crafted cover letter shows your writing skills, professionalism, dedication, and work ethic, all of which give the impression that you are genuinely interested in the role.

 **BREAKTHROUGH TIP:** Take your time tailoring your cover letter to a specific role; it is not a copy-paste regurgitation of your resume.

THE EXECUTIVE LEAP'S BREAKTHROUGH STRATEGY TO WRITE YOUR COVER LETTER

When starting a cover letter, begin with a cordial salutation. Ideally, find out the name of the hiring manager for the position or address the letter to "whom it may concern." The cover letter's first paragraph should be two to four sentences long. This is where you introduce

---

6   Doug White, "Cover Letter FAQ," Accountemps, July 23, 2014, https://www.roberthalf.com/accountemps/blog/cover-letter-faq.

yourself to the reviewer and explain how you became aware of the position.

The second paragraph should talk to the reviewer about the specific position that you're interested in. Explain the value you bring to the position and company, including several quantifiable successes from past organizations that you would bring to the role.

The third paragraph is the conclusion. Discussing the position with the reviewer, convey to him or her that you're a serious candidate for the position. You are familiar with the industry and you can bring specific, functional expertise to the organization. Ideally, research the company in advance and include in your letter a few comments specifically addressing why you want to work there.

Finally, don't go on too long; the cover letter doesn't need to be a two-page document. It needs to express your interest in the role and engage the reader—include three to four short, well-written paragraphs, then wrap it up. No fluff. Specifically showcase what you're bringing to the table. Keep it short and sweet.

If you're thinking, *Mike, it can't be that simple; cover letters must be more complicated than that!* then let me reassure you that, yes, it *is* that simple! As an example of what I mean, take a look at a few bad cover letters I've seen over the years.

BAD SAMPLE: A COVER LETTER WITH BULLET POINTS OR ODD FORMATTING

January 14, 2013

Dear Madam/Sir,

This letter and attached resume are in response to your posting for a **Director of Sales.** I am interested and well qualified to perform the responsibilities associated with this position at an extremely high degree of success and competency.

Your Requirements:	My Background:
Demonstrated success in sales management	➢ Led the $7MM EBITDA improvement of a branded specialty plastic business for XXXX by leading a team to improve selling price where appropriate, improve forecasting and focusing on higher margin opportunities. ➢ Led the 60% growth of a business for XXXX by understanding the market and changing the selling and buying habits of the organization and leading a sales team to execute the plan.
Experience managing key accounts and development of new business	➢ Responsible for XXXXXXX and XXXXXXX accounts which grew by $4MM in EBITDA for INEOS. ➢ Responsible for new business in the cosmetic and health care markets for XXXXX which generated an additional $1MM in EBITDA. ➢ Responsible for Nike and Under XXXXXX business for INVISTA which grew by $11MM in revenue.
Strong negotiation skills	➢ Developed, negotiated and administered multi-year contracts with XXXXXX that generates $17MM revenue annually. ➢ Developed, negotiated and administered sales contracts with SCXXXXX, XXXX and XXXX which all provided 5% higher than average margins and secured volumes. ➢ Developed, negotiated and executed contracts for XXXX that generate $10MM in revenue annually. ➢
Experience in plastic packaging	➢ Experience in the plastic bottle market with XXX to customers such as XXXXXX and XXXXX XXXXX. ➢ Experience in the thermoformed film market with customers such as XXXX and XXX (medical device company). ➢ Experience in the extruded film market with customers such as XXXX and XXXer.
Sales personnel management	➢ Directed 12 sales people for XXXXX to 22% growth. ➢ Directed 5 sales people and global distributors for XXXXX to $7MM margin improvement. ➢ Directed 9 sales people for XXXXA to $19MM in sales growth for XXX

I look forward to exploring this position with you further. Thank you for your kind consideration.

Best Regards,

Name Here

BAD SAMPLE: A COVER LETTER THAT DOESN'T BREATHE FOR LACK OF WHITE SPACE

COVER LETTER:

ASCENT SELECT TALENT CAPITAL

To Whom It May Concern   June 28, 2014

I would like to introduce myself for your consideration for the position your client has hired you to fill for the **Vice President – Distribution.** You were referred to me and I believe the qualifications that I possess with over 20 years of executive level Distribution/Logistics/Supply Chain experience, will exceed the requirements for the role. My experience includes executive level P&L Management and Consulting experience in the areas of Logistics, Supply Chain, 3PL, Sales, Procurement and Finance in a dozen industries but focusing in Retail, Industrial, Food and Foodservice arenas including the management of large regional and national multi-unit Distribution Networks (14 to 37 DC's - $1.2 billion to $4.5 billion). I also excel at the implementation of "best in class" innovations of logistics processes and the WMS designs needed to implement the necessary process improvements. I would also like to note my experience with merger/acquisition integration, automated warehouse systems, Multi-channel and Omni-channel e-commerce order fulfillment, WMS and TMS design/implementation expertise (including DOM), kiting, pick/pack/sort, warehouse design/construction/start-up projects (800K sq. ft.) and facilities maintenance/optimization/re-set projects (2.4 million sq. ft.) including slotting logic and inventory optimization/management incorporating statistical analytics. Coupled with all this, and perhaps most important is the hands-on personal change leadership that I have provided, while creating a team atmosphere of continuous improvement plus individual development and advancement.

As you review my resume (attached), you will ascertain that I am a distribution logistics expert that has held various executive level distribution management positions with several multi-billion dollar businesses and also formed and managed my own consulting businesses and performing in over a dozen different industries in the fields of Distribution, Logistics, Supply Chain and Business Development. I have achieved exceptional financial results in all these endeavors, while significantly improving customer service indexes and positioning the management team for continuous improvement.   I have gained the reputation of being a highly skilled logistics expert able to think "out of the box" to achieve success in a variety of situations by providing the strategic vision, tactical leadership and the change management necessary to achieve the desired profitability goals for the company.   Over the years, I have achieved outstanding results in the following disciplines:

- Excel in creating Distribution Enterprise Systems, both automated and manual and providing the necessary WMS software design upgrades needed to achieve "low cost producer" status.
- Successfully managed several of the largest distribution networks and vehicle fleets in the U.S. with annual capital expenditures of $35-$50 million
- Distribution/Logistics/WMS consulting contract achievements in a dozen different industries
- Multi-site DC/Business Unit management (11 regional to 37 national)
- Multi-Unit P&L responsibility/achievements totaling $1.5 billion to $4.2 billion in sales
- Profitable contract sales achievements with franchises and buying consortiums (Co-ops)
- KPI's exceeded industry standards for distribution (production, inventory, financials)
- Achieved highest customer service levels (CSI) for assigned Units, while reducing costs
- Merger/Acquisition Integrations (6 individual projects - from $80 million to over $600 million)
- Excel in distribution network re-engineering including required software systems re-design
- Excel in process re-engineering and the change management necessary for implementation
- Excel at team development with an emphasis on "best in class" and "sustainable competitive advantage" processes including the necessary change management leadership
- Implemented three 3PL logistical contracts for 3PL clients totaling $180 million annual revenue
- Excel at reducing costs while achieving customer satisfaction/on-time delivery ratings exceeding 99%

I sold my book of business in my consulting company and have recently completed my transitional obligations. Having assessed my options, I have determined that I am not interested in starting up another company of my own and believe that my particular skill sets will prove very beneficial to their organization given the fact that I am a proven logistic/supply chain expert who can make an immediate financial contribution to their organization. I can truly say that I am excited about this challenge as I believe that it is a perfect fit but I would also be interested in discussing other opportunities if you feel my skills would be better suited in another area. I want to thank you, in advance, for your consideration.

Respectfully Submitted,
Example Sample

GOOD SAMPLE: A COVER LETTER THAT'S JUST RIGHT

Name Sample, MBA
Address, City, ST 00112
NameSample01@gmail.com | 919-XXX-XXXX | Linkedin.com/in/namesample01

March 19, 2015

Dear Mr. Sudermann,

Recently I learned from a friend and procurement executive about a Senior Vice President of Procurement role your firm is conducting the search for. My background includes over fifteen years leading and continuously improving complex procurement, supply chain, operations, process improvement, and strategy organizations within high-growth matrix companies.

My experience as a proven top performer coupled with the unique ability to build strong coalitions, be a trusted advisor, collaborative and lead innovative change across all departments has enabled me to solve some of the companies' biggest business issues. In my current and previous roles I have streamlined processes, built first-ever procurement departments at multi-billion-dollar companies, developed a public company's first long-range strategic plan and financial models, seamlessly integrate an acquired retail chain, create and negotiated critical product and service contracts in rapidly expanding business environments, all with an entrepreneurial spirit.

Your clients need to build a strategic procurement team from the ground up, leverage spend and realize long-term reduction in costs is what I have done throughout my career. My background and expertise has been specifically within your clients industry and I am confident that my experiences can make an immediate impact.

Although secure in my current position, I am confidentially open to new executive leadership opportunities in strategic procurement and supply chain management. I welcome the opportunity to interview and look forward to hearing back from you.

Thank you,

Name Sample

Enclosure

CHAPTER 3 READER TAKEAWAYS: COVER LETTERS

- Your cover letter will most always be read in its entirety.

- Your cover letter should only be two or three paragraphs long.

- Your cover letter should be tailored for each position to include

  - the expertise and value you bring to the position and the company;

  - highlights of several key accomplishments;

  - what you know about the company and its industry; and

  - why you're interested in the role.

C H A P T E R   4

SOCIAL MEDIA

Test your social media knowledge. Circle *True* or *False*.

1. Social media has become an integral part of the process of landing a new role.

    True   *False*

2. A digital footprint is an online record of everything you look up, write, or do.

    True   *False*

3. Sixty percent of employers use social media to find you online and review your digital footprint.

    True   *False*

4. Twitter is a popular social media site for executives.

    True   *False*

5. LinkedIn was designed specifically for recruiting purposes.

    True   *False*

A positive online presence has become a must-have for candidates looking to make the executive leap. Many executives I speak with have very little and in some cases *zero* social media or online presence, so first off, know this: not having a professional online presence can be a fatal mistake.

Social media plays a critical role in your personal brand identity and acts as a conduit for people to better understand who you are and the expertise you can bring to an organization. You might think you're a superstar, but very few people outside your network know who you are. Social media provides a glimpse into the person behind the resume.

KAREN'S STORY

Recently I worked with an executive—call her "Karen"—who was reorganized out of a role she'd had for almost fifteen years. She was not ready to retire and found herself in a lurch. Her reentry into the job market is very similar to many executives who have been working for the same company for years and have thus been out of the job market.

Aside from her resume, which needed a major overhaul, she had essentially no social media presence. What do I mean by this? For starters, her LinkedIn profile was missing a professional headshot, had fewer than fifty connections, included numerous incomplete fields, and needed a substantial revamp.

During our conversations, I highlighted the significance of social media—that 60 percent of employers use social media sites to research professionals to determine if they're worthy of contacting for an open position.[7] We revamped her LinkedIn profile (we will discuss further in chapter 5) and implemented a social media strategy to assist with her landing a new role. She was an expert in her functional niche, but no one beyond her immediate network knew of her expertise.

Following my advice, she created a blog and started providing her expert opinions on several carefully selected discussion boards and forums. We wanted to make sure that when her name or a specific topic within her niche was searched, her name would appear on the first page of results, further projecting her as an expert within her niche.

She was surprised by how quickly calls started coming in from recruiters and companies inquiring about her interest in opportunities. But I wasn't surprised—nor should you be. To make the executive leap, your social media needs a breakthrough strategy. Because without the right strategy, your social media can backfire in a multitude of ways.

YOUR DIGITAL FOOTPRINT: IT'S PERMANENT

In this digital age, employers, recruiters, and anyone else for that matter, have unprecedented access to your digital footprint.

Regardless of where you are in your career, it's important for you to understand that everywhere you go online leaves a searchable record. While the digital age provides a variety of opportunities for

---

7   Amy McDonnell, "60% Employers Use Social Media to Screen Job Candidates," interviewing, April 28, 2016, http://www.interviewing.com/60-employers-use-social-media-screen-job-candidates/.

your career, when landing a new role, it can also cause irrevocable damage.

On average, 60 percent of employers use social media to find you online and review your digital footprint. Whether you're on Facebook, Twitter, LinkedIn, blogs, discussion boards, forums, or anywhere else out there, what they find will make all the difference in whether or not you receive a phone call or get deposited into "File 13."

As Karen learned, it is crucial for you to understand the impact of your online presence. Since it's difficult to anticipate the biases employers and executive recruiters are going to have toward your digital footprint, it must not differ vastly from how you represent yourself professionally. Make sure you manage your online activities very carefully.

There are important dos and don'ts to know when it comes to your online presence. **Avoid these five mistakes that most people make**.

1. **Avoid poor grammar or spelling.** Using poor grammar or spelling has tremendous negative impact. According to Jobvite, 66 percent of employers look negatively at spelling and grammar on social media.[8] Poor grammar and spelling count against you in any communication you have with a company, including your resume, cover letter, and any thank-you notes you send.

2. **Avoid inappropriate photos.** Employers often will cross-reference a professional by conducting a Facebook search. Make sure to avoid posting inappropriate or questionable photos. Also, check that you're not inappropriately tagged

8   "2014 Social Recruiting Survey," Jobvite.com, 2014, https://www.jobvite.com/wp-content/uploads/2014/10/Jobvite_SocialRecruiting_Survey2014.pdf.

in a photo on someone else's page. Nowadays on Facebook it's popular to post photos of other people from high school or college. The same with vacation photos. Your friends may tag you in a photo on their page showing you letting go on vacation. Tagged photos can come back to haunt you.

3. **Avoid controversial tweets.** Think twice about what you're tweeting. A good rule of thumb is to be deliberate about what you are writing. Say what you mean—but if you can't say something nice, at least be respectful. If you see something that catches your attention, think carefully before you retweet anything controversial.

4. **Avoid questionable contacts and associations.** Be careful whom you connect with and what associations you belong to. Connecting to radical or questionable groups won't win you any points with corporate employers.

5. **Avoid negativity.** Don't bad-mouth anyone; complaining about former employers or former coworkers or any consistent grumbling broadcast all over social media makes you look angry and retaliatory. Such public negativity is a big red flag for future employers. What's worse is that those kinds of activities can go viral, and then you really have a problem. Total unprofessionalism with a rant across social media is unacceptable. Also, do not overshare your information or overload people with too much information. This is similar to the "less-is-more" approach to your resume, discussed in chapter 2. Too much information is a turnoff.

BREAKTHROUGH TIP: Mum's the word. Don't discuss job-search details online. Recently, I found a post of someone celebrating a position they had interviewed for. Be careful about celebrating too early; making an assumption about the outcome of an interview can turn the tables against you if an employer catches wind of your announcement.

USING SOCIAL MEDIA TO YOUR ADVANTAGE

Your online presence can make a tremendous difference in your search to land your next top job. It can help separate you from other professionals, instantly elevating you, your personal brand, work experience, and expertise to a global audience. It will increase your likelihood of being seen and contacted for positions. And it can improve your chances of being considered for a call from a prospective employer. As with your resume and your cover letter, you need an executive-level social media strategy to make the executive leap.

There are a number of sites you can use to build an online social media presence. Be sure to consider using the four major social sites: Twitter, Facebook, Google+, and the must-have of them all, LinkedIn (see chapter 5). In addition, creating a blog is a great way to create content that supports your functional expertise, helps position you as an expert, and potentially enhances your online presence across the board. Finally, adding videos using YouTube or Vimeo is growing in popularity as a way to "share your smarts."

Once you've identified the sites you want to utilize, you must create online activity to be found by hiring managers and executive recruiters. Be forewarned: developing online content will be a fairly substantial investment of your time, but it's worth the investment. **Keep in mind these five breakthrough tips to make a positive impact online.**

1. **Memorability.** While you don't want to stand out online for the wrong reasons, being forgettable online is a mistake. Be sure your profiles (LinkedIn and other social media) have powerful headlines to convey who you are professionally and personally. Think of it this way: if you didn't know yourself, would your headline make you think you were someone you would want to know? More on this coming up in the next chapter, which discusses LinkedIn.

2. **Twitter.** Twitter enjoys widespread popularity today because it's inherently simple, relatively easy to use, and a quick way to build a vast community of followers. I highly recommend a Twitter account if you want to get yourself out there as an expert worth hiring. Twitter has over 270 million users, many of whom are professionals building their online presence. You can follow people, share other peoples' tweets, or send out your own messages.

   If you specialize in a specific type of function or you have a niche—maybe you're in procurement, finance, or sales—you can tweet about your area of expertise. By tweeting snippets of topics within your industry or functional niche, people will discover you are an expert and you will quickly develop a following. No matter where you are located in the world, becoming an expert on Twitter can get you noticed by very high-level people in your industry. Since Twitter is so fast moving, you can actually become an expert very quickly and begin to build your online presence. You'll even find that companies begin to follow you on Twitter.

BREAKTHROUGH TIP:

- Attach links to your Twitter bio section.
- Post often and keep posts short.
- Make posts eye-catching.
- Posts should represent your expertise and also your personality. Develop content and retweet information that would be interesting to your audience.
- Professional humor is extremely effective. Who doesn't like to smile or laugh?
- Engage your followers.
- Tweet people back if they pose a question.

3. **Facebook.** Facebook is not entirely accepted by the professional marketplace and is used sparingly by people between the ages of thirty-five and fifty-five-plus, but it still accounted for 1.65 billion active monthly users at the end of the first quarter 2016.[9] Facebook is often used by companies and recruiters to research an executive's professionalism. Don't think that just because you are connected with friends and family on Facebook that you shouldn't be professional. Inappropriate posts on Facebook have haunted many professionals. However, it is smart to leverage the power of Facebook to elevate your professional viability.

---

9   "Stats," Facebook.com newsroom, accessed July 10, 2016, http://newsroom. fb.com/company-info/.

BREAKTHROUGH TIP:

- Reference a blog or article you have written in the "About" section of your profile.
- Attach a link to your LinkedIn profile.
- Give readers a reason to come back and visit your Facebook page.
- Post interesting articles.

4. **Blogs, such as LinkedIn's Pulse.** Blogs are a great way to build a social media presence. However, blogging can be a challenge because to have any relevancy on a blog you need to post two or three articles a week. To make the most of your blogging efforts, LinkedIn has a site known as Pulse, which allows you to share your expertise through articles that you write and publish. People can read and rank the articles, and comment on your work, if you so choose. LinkedIn monitors this area of its site and has various avenues to help increase your ranking among other LinkedIn users.

    When writing articles for LinkedIn's Pulse, keep it short and sweet—three paragraphs at most. Once you post your article, Pulse will ask you if you want to post to your primary LinkedIn Group or to everyone on LinkedIn. If you have a Twitter account, you can also choose to post to both LinkedIn and Twitter, providing additional exposure.

5. **Videos.** With everyone's smartphone able to record videos, another way to broadcast your expertise is to videotape a speech or presentation. If you're presenting at a conference, for instance, have someone videotape you and put snippets

up on YouTube or Vimeo. Be sure the video posts are short and that you have the rights to post the videos.

 BREAKTHROUGH TIPS
for Using Your Smartphone to Make Videos:

- Do not shoot vertical video; all videos should be filmed in horizontal format to create a wide screen that fills the frame.

- When videotaping with an iPhone, do not use the zoom setting.

- Use a tripod. Handheld videos are inevitably shaky.

- Make sure your smartphone has the exposure lock on. This will keep a constant focus and exposure setting throughout the video and won't constantly readjust and refocus.

- Ensure the subject being videotaped is well lit. Smartphones can trick you into believing there is adequate light. You will get much better results if you purchase an inexpensive lighting kit. Even workshop lighting from Lowe's or Home Depot will do the trick. If natural light is your only option, ensure the subject is facing the light source; for instance, have the speaker face the window. Don't have a light source such as a window behind the subject as it will produce a black silhouette of the speaker.

- Ensure you have good audio. Keep the phone close to the subject (but not so close that the image is blurry) or buy an external microphone that plugs into your smartphone and place it near the subject.

CHAPTER 4 READER TAKEAWAYS: SOCIAL MEDIA

- Social media has become an integral component of the job-search process.

- Be aware of your positive and negative digital footprint.

- Don't let social media dominate your job-search endeavor.

- Sixty percent of all employers and recruiters use social media sites to cross-reference professionals they have identified to ensure worthiness for a call about a job opportunity.

- Avoid negativity and poor grammar on social media sites.

- LinkedIn, Twitter, Facebook, and Google+ are the four most popular sites used by professionals.

- For a couple hundred bucks a month, executives can have someone handle all their social media, including Twitter, Facebook, blogs, and other postings.

VISIT WWW.THEEXECUTIVELEAP.COM FOR THE LATEST STRATEGIC ADVICE ON SOCIAL MEDIA

C H A P T E R   5

YOUR LINKEDIN PROFILE

Test your LinkedIn profile knowledge. Circle *True* or *False*.

1. LinkedIn was designed as a networking tool for professionals.

    True   *False*

2. LinkedIn is used by more than 350 million people in over 200 countries and territories.

    True   *False*

3. Without a picture on LinkedIn, you are fourteen times *less* likely to be found.

    True   *False*

4. LinkedIn is a great place to showcase your expertise above and beyond your resume.

    True   *False*

5. Current and previous titles are rarely searched on LinkedIn.

    True   *False*

DON'T SKIP THIS CHAPTER!

Many executives think a LinkedIn profile is unnecessary for someone at the executive level or think they can skip LinkedIn because they don't have the time to give it any attention.

Does it surprise you to learn that an optimized LinkedIn profile is just as important for executives as it is for professionals at every other level? Essentially, employers will always want a resume but are accepting online profiles more often these days because it speeds up the hiring process, and this is why LinkedIn has become such an important part of the executive leap strategy.

And because this leading professional networking site is so important in today's executive-hiring landscape, we've devoted a whole chapter to it here.

Ninety-four percent of recruiters review a candidate's social profile before making a hiring decision.[10] It's not breaking news that LinkedIn is the top site for professionals to highlight expertise, career endeavors, and—most of all—network to find new opportunities. We know it's a great way to connect with prospective employers and employees, clients, and "friends of friends." But did you know that LinkedIn was built *for companies and executive recruiters to source and evaluate professionals*?

Once you realize LinkedIn is, foremost, *the* place where hiring managers and executive recruiters go to find talent, you'll be ahead of the competition in knowing how to construct your executive-level profile. Most executives don't know how to optimize their profile to stand out from the crowd and are missing substantial business and career opportunities.

---

10   Norberts "Jobvite: Social Recruiting is becoming a Trend," December 10, 2014, https://cake.hr/blog/social-recruiting-2013/.

On LinkedIn, there are limited instructions and blank fields—the rest is up to you. While you may not know how to fill in each of your profile's fields, hiring managers know exactly what they're looking for.

For Strategic Advice on how to build your LinkedIn profile, contact Mike at 1-844-789-LEAP, visit www.mikesudermann.com, or go to www.beyondlinkedin.com/theexecutiveleap.

That means you must use your LinkedIn profile as an opportunity to showcase you and the value you can bring to an organization. You must strategically complete your profile in order to maximize your opportunities to receive a call or message from an executive recruiter or hiring manager and stay ahead of the competition.

BREAKTHROUGH TIP: You are fourteen times more likely to be found on LinkedIn if you add your picture[11] and thirteen times more likely to have your profile viewed if you list skills.[12]

In other words: to make the leap, your LinkedIn profile needs to *always* be at its best.

What do I mean by *best*? Of course you want people—employers and recruiters—to find you. But ask yourself this: Will they review

---

11   Lisa Dougherty, "Sixteen Tips to Optimize Your LinkedIn Profile and Your Personal Brand," LinkedIn, July 8, 2014, Hahttps://www.linkedin.com/pulse/20140708162049-7239647-16-tips-to-optimize-your-linkedin-profile-and-enhance-your-personal-brand.

12   Allison Freeland, "9 LinkedIn Hacks to Boost Your Profile's Visibility," govloop, March 21, 2016, https://www.govloop.com/community/blog/9-linkedin-hacks-boost-profiles-visibility/.

your *entire* profile? Does your profile make them feel that they *must* connect? Or, an even deeper question: Do they consider you a *thought leader*?

For recruiters and hiring managers to find you, let alone inquire as to their interest in hearing about an opportunity, your LinkedIn profile must be as close to 100 percent complete as possible, compelling, and built with your personal brand in mind.

To that end, employers and recruiters can find you more easily on LinkedIn or Google searches through certain fields in your profile. It is not enough just to complete the minimum in each section of your profile. Some fields are more important than others, are more searchable, and can heavily influence LinkedIn's search results.

In this chapter, I'll explain how to build each field to your maximum advantage and make hiring managers and recruiters see you as a superstar that can make the executive leap.

Digital marketing expert Mitch Miles compiled a few LinkedIn stats revealing the connection between LinkedIn profiles and landing a top job.

- Eighty-nine percent of all recruiters have used LinkedIn to recruit someone.[13]

- Ninety-four percent of recruiters are on LinkedIn compared to 36 percent of job seekers.[14]

- Approximately 60 percent of LinkedIn users are ages thirty to sixty-four years old.[15]

13   Dan Schawbel, "How Recruiters Use Social Networks to Make Hiring Decisions Now," *Time,* July 9, 2012, http://business.time.com/2012/07/09/how-recruiters-use-social-networks-to-make-hiring-decisions-now/.
14   "2014 Jobvite Job Seeker Nation Study," Jobvite.com, 2014, http://web.jobvite.com/rs/jobvite/images/2014%20Job%20Seeker%20Survey.pdf.
15   Maeve Duggan, "The Demographics of Social Media Users," Pew Research Center, August 19, 2015, http://www.pewinternet.org/2015/08/19/the-demographics-of-social-media-users/.

- Forty-four percent of users have annual incomes of more than $75,000.[16]

- Four hundred million-plus people are on LinkedIn from more than two hundred countries and territories.[17]

- At least 128 million LinkedIn members reside in the US.[18]

- Forty-one percent of millionaires use LinkedIn.[19]

FROM GOOGLE SEARCH TO LINKEDIN

Your LinkedIn profile uses the same search-engine technology that Google uses when conducting a search. Therefore, it is critically important to create a LinkedIn profile that can be found quickly when executive recruiters and companies are searching for professionals with your expertise. Make sure your profile is optimized by completing as many fields as possible and using keywords and key phrases related to your industry and functional niche.

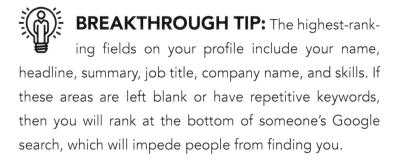 **BREAKTHROUGH TIP:** The highest-ranking fields on your profile include your name, headline, summary, job title, company name, and skills. If these areas are left blank or have repetitive keywords, then you will rank at the bottom of someone's Google search, which will impede people from finding you.

16   Ibid.

17   Craig Smith, "By the Numbers: 125+ Amazing LinkedIn Statistics," DMR Stats|Gadgets, February 25, 2016, accessed March 28, 2016, http://expandedramblings.com/index.php/by-the-numbers-a-few-important-linkedin-stats/.

18   Ibid.

19   Craig Smith, "133 Amazing LinkedIn Statistics (October 2016)," November 17, 2016, http://expandedramblings.com/index.php/by-the-numbers-a-few-important-linkedin-stats/8/.

Want to know how your LinkedIn summary and profile rank among your peers? Google yourself. LinkedIn is the social network that most often shows up at the top of Google search results. So type in your first and last name and your functional niche such as finance and see where you show up on Google. Ideally, you want to show up on the first page as close to the top as possible. The more optimized your LinkedIn profile, usually the higher you will rank on a search. I have a client who is a highly regarded and accomplished CFO. When I searched his name and functional niche, five other people with his name showed up, but not him. This tells me his profile is poorly optimized and does not have specific keywords for his areas of expertise. A look at his LinkedIn profile showed that it definitely needs work.

On the other hand, I have a COO client who *did* have a poor LinkedIn profile and vaulted to the top of the page after working with me. Together, we optimized his profile by completing the twelve must-have fields and maximizing keywords.

A common mistake is simply entering what you believe are appropriate fields and thinking you're done. However, it's a bit more strategic—by following along with the methods I present here, your profile will become a *marketing document* (like the resume) that will enable you to be found faster and more often by executive recruiters and organizations interested in your expertise, which results in potentially more interviews for you.

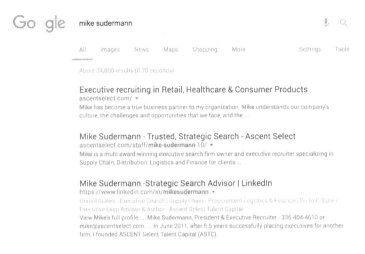

THE EXECUTIVE LEAP'S LINKEDIN PROFILE MUST-HAVES

Being found by hiring managers and executive recruiters starts with completing as many fields as possible on your LinkedIn profile. Let's start with **the top thirteen must-haves for building and optimizing an executive-level LinkedIn page**:

1. Name

2. Headline

3. Location

4. Photo

5. Summary

6. Experience

7. Titles

8. Links from LinkedIn

9. Projects

10. Skills and Endorsements

11. Interests

12. Groups

13. Education, Organizations, and Volunteering

BREAKTHROUGH TIP: Before you change your profile on LinkedIn, be sure to adjust your privacy settings. Failure to adjust this setting can (and does) lead to some embarrassing—even career-limiting—situations. Consider changing your settings so that you're anonymous when viewing other profiles as well. *See Appendix on how to adjust LinkedIn settings.*

1. **Name.** You get twenty characters for your first name and forty for your last name. I suggest you add a hyphen to your last name and add more information about you. For example: Sudermann – Strategic Search Advisor. That used only thirty-six of forty characters and now I have another option of being found on LinkedIn or a Google search.

2. **Headline.** When someone scans your LinkedIn profile, they are drawn first to your LinkedIn headline. The headline is what appears under your name. Like reading a newspaper, you read the headline first. The character limits for LinkedIn headline fields are as follows:

   • first name: twenty-character limit

   • last name: forty-character limit

   • professional headline: 120-character limit

The headline has the same essential function as the top third of the resume's first page—the space that hiring managers give six seconds to gain an impression (as discussed in chapter 2). View your headline as another place to use "city-bus marketing"; most people don't come close to maximizing the 120-character limit. Optimize the 120 characters to differentiate yourself; look to compel others to move deeper into your profile—or, even better, give you a call right away.

By default, LinkedIn populates your headline with your current employer and job title. Most people stick with the default headline. Big mistake if you want to be contacted for new opportunities. Avoid being like most people. Your headline is prime LinkedIn real estate and should be used as a descriptive headline to promote specifically what you do, share your skills and experiences, and show how you make a difference. The headline should answer "why" someone should take the next steps to dig deeper into your profile, background, and expertise.

BREAKTHROUGH TIP: To optimize your headline, add a hyphen after your last name and include your role (Mike Sudermann—Strategic Search Advisor). Adding your role to your name expands your opportunity to be found and gives you more characters to expand on in your headline.

SAMPLE LINKEDIN HEADLINES

My headline reads:

Executive Search | Supply Chain – Procurement Logistics & Finance | Dir to C-Suite | Executive Leap Advisor & Author

Other headline examples:
C-Level Executive | Transforming Organizations through Operational Change and Strategic Growth

Senior Purchasing, Procurement & Supply Chain Management Executive – Drive 100s of Millions in Savings & EBITDA Earnings

Manufacturing Leadership Expert | Executive Advisor | Front-Line Leader Developer | HR Consultant – 864-710-3783

COO | Fortune 100 | Double-Digit Sales and Earnings Growth | B2B Sales Background

Strategic Recruitment Consultant – Wireless IoT & Test 843-568-5585 | Michele@ellingtongrowthpartners.com

What would help you grow most professionally in 2017? Personal branding | Digital Marketing | LinkedIn Strategy

3. **Location.** When looking for a new role, your location is important in determining whether or not you are found by a hiring manager or a recruiter. When a search is conducted on LinkedIn, location is almost always searched first, as companies typically want local talent. If you are willing to relocate to a specific city, then put that location in your profile.

For instance, I received a resume from a woman in Portland who wanted to relocate to Kansas City. Her resume was on the right track, listing her parent's house, a Kansas City address, in the top third. However, while the address on her resume showed Kansas City, when I reviewed her LinkedIn profile the location was Portland. Make sure your location matches across all platforms.

Executive recruiters and hiring managers will always search for talent locally first. If you prefer to remain open to relocation, then you can indicate your location as the United States (zip code 00000)

4. **Photo.** I highly recommended that you add a photo to your LinkedIn page. A close-up (headshot) of you in professional attire on a plain background is best. For professionals looking to get hired, a photo works better than an avatar (a digital image). Whether you include a photo or an avatar, a LinkedIn profile is only considered complete when you upload an image into the profile's photo space. A complete profile allows you to connect with more people—40 percent more people, according to LinkedIn.[20]

BREAKTHROUGH TIP: Listing your industry in the field under your headline will help in how quickly you will be found.

5. **Summary.** With two thousand characters at your disposal, your LinkedIn summary is where you differentiate yourself from your peers. Don't do what everyone else does and copy-paste your resume into the summary field. The summary is your brochure,

---

20 "Profile Completeness," LinkedIn, accessed March 28, 2016, https://www.linkedin.com/static?key=pop%2Fpop_more_profile_completeness.

where you *showcase* what you *do*, what you *know*, what you *are looking to do*, and the *value you bring* to an organization.

The first line of the summary should be a shout-out about your expertise. For example, *chief operating officer.* Then mention the industries you've worked in, such as *healthcare, retail,* and *food manufacturing.*

Next, speak about the value you bring. Similar to your resume's key accomplishments, mention how much money you have saved (provide specific numbers), what sort of revenues you've generated (percentages), and processes you have improved.

Most people write their summary in first person. Make sure to include keywords, key phrases, and acronyms associated with your expertise. Lastly, tell people exactly how to reach you by including your e-mail address and cell phone number.

 ### BREAKTHROUGH TIP:

- Give people an option of downloading your entire profile—a great takeaway. Go to "View profile as," click "Save to PDF," then go to your Summary and add the PDF.

- Just as with your resume, make sure your profile has three or four keywords or phrases that are relevant to your area of expertise, which help your name get picked up when someone performs an online search. (Refer to *Appendix B* for more keywords.)

SAMPLE LINKEDIN SUMMARY

ASCENT Select | Strategic Search Advisors | Unique | Customized, Collaborative Results

Flat Fees | Double Placement Guarantee!! | Candidates in 10-days | 100% Acceptance Rate
500 Locations | 30 Countries

Mike Sudermann, President & Executive Recruiter - 336-404-4610 or mike@ascentselect.com

Retail / Multi-Channel (Franchise, Licensed, Privately Held), Healthcare, Fitness / Wellness, Consumer Products, Distribution / Logistics, Banking and Private Equity

RECENT PLACEMENTS: CEO, CFO, SVP Finance, VP Strategic Sourcing, Director of Procurement, CIO, Sr. Mgr. Procurement and VP HR

A Sample of our Clients Includes; LFUSA, Ascena Retail Group, Billabong, Sundial Brands, Bond Mfg., Global Brands Group, Crystal Farms, Beacon Health Options, The Men's Wearhouse, Frye Boots

231 Direct Hire Placements since 2011

What makes ASCENT SELECT unique?
1. We visit all our clients - on our dime!
2. Flat Fee's
3. Double Placement Guarantee - Very Unique - No Firm matches this guarantee!!!
4. Leading Edge Assessments – Conducted at NO Charge!
5. We meet all candidates presented –face-to-face
6. Present Candidates in 10-days or less
7. Team of veteran executive search partner's available 24/7
8. Global network on 6 continents / 500 Locations / 1300 Recruiters
9. 100% of our searches are filled! We work in acceptances only not offers!

In June 2011, I founded ASCENT Select Talent Capital (now known as ASCENT Select). The mission was simple, provide executive search services with a Unique "Strategic Search Advisor" approach while substantially raising the search services bar well beyond what other typical recruiters provide.

Mike specializes in All Things Supply Chain and Finance

ASCENT Select has 7 affiliate executive search partners with multiple years experience within IT, Engineering, Operations, IoT, Sales, and Legal.

ADDITIONAL SERVICES: Project Based Recruiting, Outplacement, GEO, Background Checks, and Executive Marketing (fee based)

6. **Experience.** This is an opportunity to write about specific experiences, projects, and achievements with a specific employer. Use your maximum of two thousand characters to talk about your expertise and successes. In chapter 6 you will learn about the FAB© worksheet, and you can use that information to help write your experience descriptions for each role. The key is to make it different from your summary and your resume while still using keywords and key phrases.

7. **Titles.** These include current and previous positions. These fields are located in the experience section and are critically important to complete. You get one hundred characters, and while you may think that just writing "VP of IT" or "CFO" is enough, that'd be a huge mistake. The LinkedIn algorithm ranks these fields as more often searched than any other fields—executive recruiters and hiring managers almost always search titles first. Furthermore, don't feel as though you have to write out vice president. LinkedIn sees VP or vice president as the same, so you can save characters by abbreviating.

SAMPLE TITLE FIELD

Executive Recruiter | All Things Supply Chain, Distribution, Logistics, Finance – Manager to C-Suite

... Versus these other titles I found on LinkedIn: "Associate Director"—of what? "Marketing & Technology"—of what? These are titles that provide zero value. You get one hundred characters—maximize the value!

8. **Links from LinkedIn.** You can provide up to three different links to other websites' landing pages on your LinkedIn profile.

Links offer the perfect opportunity for people who are interested in learning more about you to visit an outside website—such as a page containing your resume, a white paper or e-book, or a separate blog. When creating these links, label them something more interesting than "my website" or "Read my blog." For instance, the hotlink on my page reads "Mike's book—*The Executive Leap*."

9. **Projects**. List any projects you have worked on in the past and include numbers to demonstrate the level of success you achieved. A great idea is to list your company first followed by the specific company, project, and results—if you have space. The Project Name field gets 255 characters so you can utilize this space with additional keywords and info to describe a project in the title.

SAMPLE PROJECT TITLE FIELD

Global Brands Group (f.k.a. LFUSA) Subsidiary of Li & Fung, - World's Leading Retail Sourcer & Logistics Co. I ASCENT Select Built North Carolina's Finance, Operations, IT, HR, Customer Service & Legal - Over 160 Placements

10. **Skills and Endorsements.** LinkedIn provides plenty of additional opportunities to expand on your experience and expertise throughout the profile. Take advantage of these additional fields to further detail what you can bring to a prospective employer:

   - **Skills.** You're allowed to select fifty skills that demonstrate your expertise. You can arrange your top-ten skills in a rank order and then list another forty skills.

- **Endorsements.** Once you have selected your skills, LinkedIn users can endorse you based on that specific skill. Endorsements, like keywords, increase your search visibility. According to LinkedIn, the more endorsements you get on skills, the more often you will appear in search results.

11. **Interests**. Why are these important? Recently our firm had a client specifically ask us to find a controller who likes to fish for bass or snowboard. We found a controller who loves to snowboard and also happened to fit the client's position requirements, along with being a good cultural fit. He was offered the job.

    Your interests, whether you like to fish, snowboard, or dance the tango, can help you land a job. Don't lose out on opportunities because you didn't complete a field on your LinkedIn profile.

12. **Groups.** Being an active participant in a LinkedIn group is a significant step to gaining recognition as a thought leader. While there are over two million groups to choose from, LinkedIn limits you to fifty. Join at least one and create discussions that are in your industry niche, are interesting or engaging, and compel a reader to comment. Showcase your expertise. The point of being active is to drive traffic to your profile. The more engaged you are, the more opportunities you'll have come your way.

    For instance, if your expertise is finance, comment on a post on LinkedIn. You can thank the person for sharing and you can add value to the post by sharing your expertise on the subject. You can also share a group member's post with your network—like paying it forward—which always pays back huge dividends.

Recently there was an article posted on my LinkedIn profile. I added a few comments and shared it with my LinkedIn network and on Twitter. This single article (which I didn't write) ended up boosting my weekly profile reviews by 5 percent; in addition, I received numerous positive comments. Participating in groups is a great way to keep your name and expertise front and center.

13. **Education, Organizations, and Volunteering**. Be sure to complete these fields. LinkedIn reports that members who list a school in their profile get seven times more views, and one in five managers hired an individual because of their volunteer experiences.

Bottom line: the more complete your LinkedIn profile, the more often you will be searched, found, and identified for your expertise as it relates to new job opportunities.

CONNECTIONS

The number of connections seems to always be front and center when it comes to a LinkedIn Profile. But are they really that important? LinkedIn's algorithm places importance on people who are closest to you, or first-degree connections, so from that standpoint, connections are important—but there is no magic number of connections to strive for on LinkedIn.

It is more important to optimize your profile fields and your *engagement*. What do I mean by engagement? If you haven't posted articles or replied to articles on LinkedIn, then do so! This makes a big difference. How involved are you in your groups? And have you optimized your profile?

BEYOND THE THIRTEEN PROFILE MUST-HAVES

As discussed at the beginning of this chapter, most executive-level LinkedIn pages go beyond the basics to present the professional as a thought leader. To learn more about advanced LinkedIn tools and tips and how to reposition your page to become a thought leader in your industry, visit www.theexecutiveleap.com, contact Mike directly at 1-844-789-LEAP, or connect with Mike on LinkedIn; he welcomes all requests.

CHAPTER 5 READER TAKEAWAYS: YOUR LINKEDIN PROFILE

- LinkedIn is the number-one social media site for professionals between thirty and sixty-four years of age.

- LinkedIn was *not* designed for professionals to search for jobs but rather for employers and recruiters to search for you.

- Fully completed LinkedIn profiles will maximize how you rank and how quickly people can find you.

- LinkedIn headlines have 120 characters. Be sure to use all of them.

- The summary section allows for two thousand characters. Don't copy and paste your resume.

- Differentiate yourself in the summary by starting with your title and niche and wrap up with keywords, specialization, and skills.

- Turn off profile notifications when making changes to your LinkedIn profile.

- Regularly comment and share to be an active participant in groups.

FOR MORE INFORMATION ON HOW TO BUILD YOUR PROFILE AND OPTIMIZE YOUR VISIBILITY, VISIT THEEXECUTIVELEAP.COM

C H A P T E R 6

INTERVIEW PREP

Test your interview-preparation knowledge. Circle *True* or *False*.

1. Differentiating yourself from other candidates starts when you receive a phone call to interview.

    True   *False*

2. Taking notes during an interview will help position you as a number-one must-hire.

    True   *False*

3. You should always wear cologne or perfume to an interview.

    True   *False*

4. First impressions will make or break an interview.

    True   *False*

5. You should always take a separate page of references to a face-to-face interview.

    True   *False*

You've created your executive-level resume, sent it in with a cover letter, and updated your social media presence and LinkedIn profile based on my proven breakthrough strategies. Then you get the phone call. The voice on the other line says, "We're interested in learning more about you. Can you come in for an interview on Monday?"

Congratulations—you're now a *candidate*!

You think to yourself, *Excellent, time to prepare.*

Wrong. You should have started your preparation *prior* to the interview invitation. What do I mean? From the beginning of the interview process, the ultimate goal is to differentiate yourself from all other candidates; this starts with nailing the invitation call, then goes right into strategically preparing for the interview so that you can ultimately position yourself as the top candidate and make the executive leap.

BREAKTHROUGH TIP: During or immediately after that first phone call, most candidates (i.e., your competition) start trying to figure out how to get two days off work next week to go to an interview, when to go to the dry cleaners, get a haircut, travel, and other logistics—meanwhile, they spend zero amount of time preparing for the interview. Don't be like your competition.

Now that you have the opportunity to interview, you need to be more than a candidate; you must *be the executive* they're looking to hire. Planning ahead for interviews starts long before getting the call. It is all in the prep work.

In this chapter I will discuss what specific prep work needs to be completed to answer the following questions:

- You get the call, now what?

- What strategies can you employ for phone, video, and face-to-face interview success?

- What are the best ways to position yourself as the number-one must-hire and leap over the competition?

We'll dive into the invitation call's follow-up questions that most executives fail to ask, tips for both phone- and video-interview success, note-taking strategies (including the FAB worksheet), what to bring to the face-to-face, and how to make the best first impression.

I know you may be thinking, *What can Mike tell me about interviewing that I don't already know? Heck, I'm a CFO, I'm successful, I've got it covered.* While all that is true, in my experience, a *good* interview can likely get you the national average compensation increase of 15 percent. A *great* interview can help you secure 25, 30, 40—maybe even 50 percent more than you are currently making.

THE INVITATION CALL

While receiving an interview invitation is an exciting moment, think of it as an information-gathering step. Hiring managers and executive recruiters should always provide you details and logistics of the interview. If, however, you are not getting this information, then ask for it.

You'd be surprised how many executives forget or simply don't ask for details when receiving a call directly from a company. Flubbing the invitation call can derail you right out of the gate. Once selected for an interview, your primary goal every step of the interview process is to make a lasting and positive impression on everyone you meet with.

PAT'S STORY

Pat, an executive looking to make a discreet job change, received a phone call from a company representative wanting to set up a phone interview. Pat accepted the invitation—a phone call for Tuesday at 10:45 a.m.—and excitedly hung up the phone. He was thrilled to share the good news with me. When I asked him a series of follow-up questions (we'll get to those in a minute), and he could not come up with a single answer, he immediately realized he knew nothing about the scheduled phone interview other than the date and time. Even for the actual role, he only knew what he had been told by his friend who referred him into the company. Therefore, Pat was unable to prepare in such a way that would enable him to differentiate himself from other candidates the company was interviewing. He was completely in the dark, and as a result, even though he said the interview "went well," he was not invited back to continue the interview process. He failed from the get-go to differentiate himself from the competition, and he paid the price.

BREAKTHROUGH TIP: It's called "the interview *process*" for a good reason. The many steps and length of time interviewing takes often make it seem like an endurance race rather than a sprint. Wherever you are in the process, always keep in mind your ultimate goal: to constantly differentiate yourself as the number-one must-hire. Make it a no-brainer for the organization to make you an offer. Do this and you'll exceed the national average in compensation and successfully make the leap.

In order to position yourself as the number-one must-hire, you must make sure to garner as much control over the interview situation as possible. Ideally, you want the company to fall head-over-heels in love with you as quickly as possible. Pat's mistake during the invitation call was that he failed to get any additional information about the interview: the role of the person he was going to be speaking with, whether or not anyone else was going to be involved, the expected length of the call, and more. Don't make the same mistake. Regardless of whether you receive an e-mail or phone call inviting you to an interview, you must always set yourself apart from the competition.

 **BREAKTHROUGH TIP:** When receiving an invitation to interview, make sure you get the answers to the following **top-ten invitation questions:**

1. What type of interview is it? Phone, video, or face-to-face?

2. Who am I meeting with? Is this person the hiring manager? If not, what is the interviewer's role with the company?

3. Who *is* the hiring manager (get a name), and what is his or her title?

4. Where is the interview? What day and what time?

5. If travel is involved, what are the particulars?

6. Who will initiate the call (if a phone interview)—the interviewer or me? If me, what number do I call?

7. What is the initiator's phone and e-mail, just in case an issue comes up?

8. Who else will be in on the call? (Get names and titles.)

9. How long is the interview expected to take (so that you can plan your schedule accordingly)?

10. What are next steps following the call?

Before hanging up the phone, verify that you have all the correct numbers and whether you are dialing a direct line or calling in on a conference line that includes a PIN number. If you are receiving the call, make sure the interviewer has your correct phone number.

Lastly, to avoid time-zone confusion, reconfirm the time of the call for both parties; for instance, you may be in eastern standard time and the interviewer may be in central daylight time. Is the interview at 10:00 a.m. central or eastern time? I can honestly say that I hear about calls getting screwed up every single day. This is a common mistake that can easily be avoided.

BREAKTHROUGH TIP: Getting the answers on what to expect enables you to go into the interview well prepared. Researching the *people* you will be interviewing with is a given—especially for seasoned executives. Preparing *emotionally*, however, is not always done—but it is something I highly recommend as part of interview preparation. The psychology of visualizing success is very real. According to John Kehoe, known for his pioneering work in mind power and the author of *Mind Power Into the 21st Century*, "the subconscious mind cannot distinguish between what is real and what is imagined. Your subconscious will act upon the images you create within, regardless of whether those images reflect your current reality or not."[21] Run through the interview in your head. Visualize success.

THE EXECUTIVE LEAP'S BREAKTHROUGH STRATEGY FOR PHONE-INTERVIEW SUCCESS

Most companies prefer to conduct telephone interviews before meeting in person. If a phone interview sounds easy enough not to prepare for ahead of time, don't be fooled; what's *actually* easy at this point is making a fatal mistake that can cost you the job.

Follow my **three-part breakthrough strategy for phone-interview success**.

1. Take the telephone interview at home, not on a cellphone or in the car on the way to an event. Telephone interviews are usually the precursor to a face-to-face interview, and they can make or break you.

2. Unless the interview is a video teleconference, the interviewer can't see you, but he or she can still make certain assumptions about you by the tone of your voice—I'm sure you've discovered for yourself that you can hear a person smile over the phone. So smile!

3. Stand up during a phone interview. Consider the phone interview to be similar to an athletic competition. When

---

21   John Kehoe, "Visualization," http://www.learnmindpower.com/ using_mindpower/visualization/.

you're standing up, your diaphragm is full of air. You will have more energy and will come across as more actively engaged. If you're sitting down or distracted or having an otherwise not-so-great day, you'll project negativity in your voice over the phone.

TAKING NOTES: THE FAB SHEET

In today's climate of interviewing, candidates must prepare research notes in advance *and* take notes during the interview. Companies want to hire people who are interested in joining their organization. Taking notes shows interest in what the interviewer is discussing.

After a decade of experience, I've found the best strategy for taking notes in an interview is to build them around what I call the FAB sheet—features, accomplishments, and benefits—see Appendix C for an example. The FAB is a comprehensive inventory of specific career accomplishments that will help you prepare for any interview. Don't do what 95 percent of your competition is doing—regurgitating what is already on their resumes. This provides zero value and will immediately derail you. To best prepare, complete the FAB and then transfer key components to the FAB summary.

Ahead of the interview, insert the FAB summary under two or three blank pages in a legal pad. The blank pages are necessary, in essence, to help you retain a level of discretion while you're taking notes, especially should you step away from the interview for a tour or some other reason.

The FAB goes into extensive detail, and while it is important to complete the FAB—because it will substantially improve how you interview—you may want to select specific accomplishments and benefits for each position. Make sure that under "accomplishments" in your FAB summary, you include the big three—what you've *saved* a company, how much you've *made* for a company, or what processes you *improved*—and then think beyond those to other achievements, such as awards, publications, or patents.

While listing your accomplishments, also branch out and list specific benefits you can bring to the organization. Use the bottom and back of the FAB summary to take notes.

In addition to the FAB summary, for each person you're interviewing with, you'll need to prepare tailored questions—and spaced far enough apart on the page to write down answers. If interviewing with multiple people, make sure you have a separate page of questions for each person with enough space for notes. I know this seems silly to discuss, but these simple note-taking strategies will pay off in major dividends at the end of the interview process. Ahead in chapter 8, I'll share with you what I call "meat-on-the-bone" questions that I guarantee your competition will not be asking. These questions will help position you as the number-one must-hire.

BREAKTHROUGH TIP: When in a group interview where you're meeting with two or three people at the same time, first—right after you sit down—draw a quick seating chart. It can be a circle or a square with the first and last names of the individuals in each of the seats. This will allow you to respond to questions accordingly. The last thing you want to happen is to be caught in the middle of an interview and have forgotten someone's name. Make the chart near the bottom edge of the page so that you can discreetly refer to it if needed and still easily flip through your pages of notes.

Taking notes may seem like a rudimentary idea, but I have a client who recently disqualified a candidate who came in for a face-to-face interview without a notepad or pen. He took zero notes during the first two hours of interviews. Here is the kicker: he was the number-one candidate, and the company actually had him scheduled for over five hours of interviews with the entire team—but when his lack of note-taking gave the impression that he was not interested in learning about the company, he was dismissed early.

Bottom line: Always take a portfolio with a notepad *and use it*. Doodle for the entire time if need be, but at least make it look like you are interested enough by taking notes.

FRED'S STORY

Fred spent his entire life in meetings. For years, his colleagues witnessed and admired him for taking copious notes. One day, about twenty-five years into his

career, someone discovered that he was actually doodling. There were some notes but mostly just doodles. Don't get me wrong, Fred was a great listener, but it turns out that he was also a fantastic artist and often incorporated his notes into his doodles. Fortunately for Fred there were no reper-

Fred Sudermann and his "City Scape."
See more of Fred's artwork at
theexecutiveleap.com

cussions—only that all his colleagues wanted his art. So much so that he started making doodle art in his spare time. His doodles were amazingly colorful. He doodled on everything, even three-dimensional objects.

By the time he retired from a highly respected executive career, he had amassed a fantastic collection of doodle art. Some were selling in a local store, some were permanently placed on the organization's campus, and some were even featured in art museums around the city. So again, take real notes or doodle—but whatever you do, make sure the people you are meeting with *think* you are totally engaged in their conversation.

THE EXECUTIVE LEAP'S BREAKTHROUGH STRATEGY FOR VIDEO-INTERVIEW SUCCESS

Companies increasingly use video-conferencing interviews as a way to get to know a candidate better than by phone. If you are invited to a video interview, keep this five-part breakthrough strategy in mind to make a positive first impression.

1. **Dress just like you are going to a normal face-to-face interview**. Top to bottom. A few years ago, an executive candidate attended a video interview wearing a shirt, coat, and tie on top—and shorts on the bottom. The hiring manager could see the shorts and disqualified the candidate immediately, saying, "His lack of dress was lazy and disrespectful."

2. **Do a test run one day prior to the interview.** Where are you going to sit and what will the interviewer see behind you? Remove from the background inappropriate

photographs, art, mirrors, or anything that may cause a distraction. Check your lighting, and if there's not enough, put a light behind you, not in front of you. Practice the video call with a friend to be sure all systems work.

3. **Don't use your cellphone for the video call.** If using your own computer, ensure that the computer camera is at eye level. Ideally, go to an office center that offers video-conferencing for the call. When interviewing, be sure to look at the camera or just above it.

4. **Give the interviewer your attention**. Make sure your room is quiet. Close your windows, and seal off the room from exterior noise—kids, pets, landscapers, passing sirens, etc. Turn off your cellphone. And don't surf the web while on the call.

5. **Prepare your answers**. Be prepared to answer questions by having notes, questions, and your FAB summary in front of you.

WHAT TO BRING WITH YOU TO THE FACE-TO-FACE INTERVIEW

I'll talk more about the actual face-to-face interview in chapter 8, but when preparing ahead of time for the interview, make sure to put together the following items:

1. **A portfolio that includes a pad of paper and several pens.** You need to take notes.

2. **FAB summary**.

3. **Written questions** for each person you're meeting with. We will discuss specific questions to ask in chapter 8.

4. **Two to three copies of your printed resume on high-quality paper.** It's common for interviewers to show up to the interview without your resume, and oftentimes people are asked to participate in the interview who were not originally scheduled, so you'll want to have extra copies available.

5. **A snack, necessary medications, and a bottle of water.** Companies sometimes forget that a candidate has been interviewing nonstop for hours. Don't find yourself in one of those Snickers candy-bar ads where Marsha from *The Brady Bunch* turns into an angry caveman because she is starving.

    View the face-to-face interview as an athletic event. You wouldn't spend hours running, playing golf, or exercising without water and a snack. Do not count on the company to provide snacks or meals unless noted on an itinerary.

6. **Business cards.** Even if you're unemployed, have some made. You're an executive, so don't go cheap on flimsy cards. You want to make a good impression, so use decent card stock that allows you to print front and back. List your core competencies on the back.

7. **Thank-you note cards.** I have worked with thousands of professionals on interview strategies, and the simple strategy of delivering a handwritten thank-you note to a receptionist following an interview will absolutely differentiate you from the competition. Bring four or five note cards and envelopes with you (nice ones, not cheap stuff). After you wrap up the interview and leave the company's premises,

find a quiet place to sit down and write notes to the people you just met. This makes a fantastic positive impression because most candidates are lazy and just send an e-mail.

BREAKTHROUGH TIP: Use your notes from the interview to write a short thank-you note to your interviewer(s), then hand deliver the notes back to the receptionist or drop them in the mail on the way out of town so they arrive the following day. Keep the note simple. I have clients who have disqualified candidates for excessively long thank-you notes or those that have poor grammar and misspellings. Short is better.

8. **References.** Although references are not typically included on resumes anymore, when bringing your resume to a face-to-face interview, I recommend you also bring multiple copies of references in a separate document. Make sure to alert your references that they may receive a call. Each individual reference should include a full name, cellphone number, e-mail, and your relationship to the person.

By the time you have made it to the face-to-face interview, you typically have had at least one or two phone interviews (and perhaps a video interview). At this stage, a printed resume and a page of references in-hand is your way of showing the interviewer you are always prepared (think Girl Scout or Boy Scout). The references can work to garner additional influence with the hiring manager or other executives interviewing you—especially if you and an interviewer have a mutual connection, which is often the case.

BOB'S STORY

Bob was a candidate of mine for a chief procurement officer role. He had made it to the face-to-face interviews and along the way had learned that the hiring manager used to work with an executive who Bob also knew. This executive, a recognized industry leader, was one of Bob's references. As he prepared for the interview, I advised Bob to add a separate sheet of references to include with his resume.

What is important here is the *separate sheet*. Let's say Bob hands his resume to the interviewer and she says she already has it. Bob can then say, "Please take this sheet, as it contains my references." Bob will do that with everyone in the interview process. Ideally, the hiring manager will call Bob's reference to chat about old times and discuss Bob. This helped him go from being a candidate who loosely matched the specs of the role on paper to one of the top candidates in consideration for the role out of over twenty. What was the breakthrough strategy in this case? **A separate page of references presented to each person he interviewed with.**

YOUR APPEARANCE: REMEMBER YOUR TEETH!

After all the work you've done on your resume and in conducting a winning telephone interview, you certainly don't want to blow it by showing up with an appearance that sends the wrong message. Here are some tips for showing the company that you are ready to make the executive leap from the moment you walk in the door.

BREAKTHROUGH TIP: First impressions can oftentimes make or break you as a candidate. Are you a serious candidate? Do you fit culturally? These are questions going through an interviewer's mind when he or she meets you face-to-face the first time. While it has been said that an interviewer will make a hiring decision in the first sixty to ninety seconds, according to an article in *Business Insider*, you really only have seven seconds to make a good first impression[22]—so make it count.

- **Gentlemen, facial hair will grow back**. Where interviews are concerned, not going in clean-shaven can be a big risk. I've had clients who don't allow facial hair (beards or mustaches) of any kind. Make sure you know what the company policy is prior to going in for the interview, and if you don't know, shave.

- **Ladies, don't overdo the makeup**. Ladies, you know what I mean.

- **Do your hair.** For men, get your haircut a day or two before an interview.

- **Consider your jewelry from the neck up.** You wouldn't think an executive would have visible piercings, but in today's world, I have seen it all. Men should remove all piercings, and women should wear conservative jewelry.

---

22   Anna Pitts, "You Only Have 7 Seconds To Make A Strong First Impression," *Business Insider*, April 8, 2013, http://www.businessinsider.com/only-7-seconds-to-make-first-impression-2013-4.

- **Nix the cologne or perfume.** Scents can trigger powerful emotions, and some people are allergic to cologne or perfume. One candidate I sent in for an interview was wearing the same cologne as the interviewer's ex-significant other, which triggered a negative memory in her; it was a huge distraction, and needless to say, the interview was over before it even began.

- **Clip your nails**. Short and neat. No need for over-the-top nail polish.

- **Brush your teeth**. This is especially necessary if you have had a meal beforehand. If you do decide to eat before the interview, eat clean food—nothing too pungent like garlic or onions—and don't drink alcohol.

- **Be sure your clothes are clean and pressed**. If the shirt or blouse is tattered or stained, opt for a new one.

- **Polish your shoes**. Ladies, a slight heel is preferable to sky-high heels or flats.

- **Wear dark socks**. No white socks with black trousers and black shoes!

- **Sleep.** Get a good night's sleep. You should not attend an interview looking like you stayed up all night or are hung over.

- **Use a firm handshake.** I know some of these tips sound silly, but they're common mishaps. You don't have to squeeze the other person's hand off—one quick squeeze and you're good. I've had executives be immediately disqualified based on a weak handshake.

- **Remember your teeth!** Last but not least—an executive-search consultant friend of mine sent a candidate in for an interview who showed up *without* his two front teeth. Imagine an executive walking into an interview dressed to the nines, shoes polished, pressed shirt, portfolio in hand—and when he starts talking his two front teeth are missing! Turns out he was an ex-hockey player who had lost them in a game a number of years prior. He forgot to put them in that morning when getting ready for the interview. Client and candidate laughed it off and eventually he was hired—but it was one heck of a first impression.

DRESS FOR SUCCESS

Unless otherwise told by the company what to wear for the interview, a candidate should always dress up. My firm had a candidate interviewing over the holidays for a general counsel role. He showed up wearing a tie with martini glasses and Christmas lights on it. His shirt cuffs were ratty and his shoes were not polished. He didn't seem to put any effort into how he presented himself. Again, first impressions can make or break you.

While your attire is not a measure of how successful you are as a candidate or how you will ultimately fit a role, it is a sign of respect given to the interviewers who are taking time out of their day to meet with you. Your interview attire shows how serious you are about the opportunity. Men should always go conservative: wear a charcoal or navy-blue suit and a white or light-blue shirt. Even if the company is casual and wears jeans and polo shirts, you should still wear dark trousers and a sport coat (you can always remove your jacket).

Likewise, women should wear a dark business suit and appropriately colored blouse. If you opt for a skirt, keep it at a conservative length.

©Glasbergen
glasbergen.com

"I *am* dressed for success! Of course, my idea of success may not be exactly the same as yours."

BREAKTHROUGH TIP: Unless the interviewer specifically tells you there's no need to wear a suit, don't opt for slacks and a polo shirt in an interview for a C-suite position. Even if the company manufactures $250 worn and faded jeans, don't assume that's the attire worn by the company's executives!

DINING RULES

Going out to eat can turn an interview into a dangerous situation. Here are three general rules to follow when meeting clients for a meal.

1. *No alcohol!* Do not drink alcohol, even if told it is okay by the person you are meeting with. If the person insists, it is recommended you only have one glass of wine or beer and stay away from the hard liquor.

2. No sloppy foods. Avoid foods that stain (i.e., spaghetti, meatball sandwiches, ribs, etc.) and, basically, anything that takes more than one napkin. Remember Murphy's Law—anything that can go wrong, will go wrong, and at the worst possible moment. It's just not worth the risk.

3. Redeem the time. Meeting a hiring manager for a meal is 50 percent business and 50 percent just getting to know you. Take advantage of the time to learn about the city, schools, industry, and company culture.

BREAKTHROUGH TIP: *Turn off your cellphone.* If your cellphone rings during an interview, you're not doing yourself any favors. Leave it in the car or turn it to silent—not buzz.

CHAPTER 6 READER TAKEAWAYS:
INTERVIEW PREP

BEFORE THE INTERVIEW

- Ask my ten follow-up questions when invited for an interview.
- Use the FAB sheet and FAB summary to prepare discussion points about the features, accomplishments, and benefits you bring to an organization.
- Check out Appendix E for the pre-interview checklist.

TELEPHONE INTERVIEWS

- Stand up when talking. Be engaged and energetic.
- Keep water handy.
- Be positive. Smile.

FACE-TO-FACE INTERVIEWS

- **Nourishment:** Take a snack and water.
- **Dress for success:** Press your clothes. Shine your shoes.
- **Men:** Wear a suit and tie (no crazy ties) and a white or light-blue shirt. And shave.
- **Women:** Wear a dark business suit and low heels (not flats).

- **Piercings:** Women should wear conservative earrings. Men/women—no eyebrow, lip, nose, tongue, chin, or cheek studs or rings.

- Firm handshake. No cologne or perfume.

- **Remember your teeth!**

C H A P T E R   7

TRICK-OR-TRAP QUESTIONS

Test your trick-or-trap question knowledge. Circle *True* or *False*.

1. Some interviewers will do all they can to derail you as a candidate.

    True   *False*

2. The question, "What is your ideal job?" is a trick question.

    True   *False*

3. "What are your greatest strengths?" is not a trick question.

    True   *False*

4. The best way to answer the question, "Why should I hire you?" is to provide a list of your qualifications that best fit into the role.

    True   *False*

5. The best way to answer a question targeted toward a weakness is by confirming you don't have that experience.

    True   *False*

The interview often takes unexpected turns when it comes to the questions posed to candidates. Interviewers come in three varieties: (1) the one who was passed up for the promotion and comes in armed and dangerous, looking for ways to derail you; (2) the one who was asked last minute to attend the interview due to someone being absent—this person has no interest in taking time out of his or her schedule and sees this as a total waste of time, asking questions on the fly; (3) the one who has a stake in the hiring decision and interviews you with scripted questions and is savvy about the interview process.

No matter who interviews you, you *will* get hit with a trick question or two. The good news is that for each question, there's an answer to help you leap the competition. Having been in this business for a number of years now, I've amassed a list of more than sixty questions that can catch you completely off guard if you are not careful. For each question, I have an answer that helps position you in the best light possible.

> I've listed more than forty questions on www.mikesudermann. com/trickortrapquestions.

To make the executive leap, it's important to have an idea of what some of these questions are and how to provide the best answer. Ahead are strategies and answers to **ten breakthrough trick-or-trap questions.**

Question #1: What is your ideal company, location, and job?

This question will come from someone who is an experienced interviewer and thinks you are overqualified for the role. Instead of showing her hand directly, she uses the question to let the candidate reveal the answer.

If you're coming from a well-known or admired company, industry, larger city, or larger role, the interviewer is most likely feeling defensive and thinking you might consider them a second-rate or bush-league company. Therefore, you must go out of your way to make them feel at ease by expressing genuine enthusiasm for the position and credible reasons why you will be happy to come from a larger organization and move from New York City to Little Rock, Arkansas.

Question #2: What are your greatest strengths?

As a candidate, you don't want to come across as egotistical or arrogant, but you don't want to appear *too* humble either. Ideally, by the time you receive this question, you've already identified your interviewer's primary wants or needs from you as a candidate.

To be ready for this question, prepare a mental list of your strengths in your head prior to the interview. Think of examples that illustrate those strengths. For instance, if you uncover during the interview that the company is looking for cross-functional leadership and you have that experience, then talk about one of your strengths as being a cross-functional leader.

Base your answer on what you discover early in the interview (more on that in chapter 8), on research you performed beforehand, or on the fact that there are ten traits that all employers love to have in their employees.

THE EXECUTIVE LEAP'S TEN MOST DESIRABLE TRAITS:

1. Honesty and integrity

2. A good fit with corporate culture

3. Great communication skills

4. Dedication or a willingness to go above and beyond what it would normally take to achieve excellence in the organization

5. Clear goals

6. Enthusiasm and motivation for what you're doing within the company

7. Confident, healthy leadership

8. A proven track record of achievements—what you have done for a company that saved money, made money, or improved a process

9. Adding value and achieving great things within the organization

10. Intelligence or management savvy

Question #3: Why are you leaving your current company? Why did you leave your previous company?

The interviewer is looking for your motivation and patterns in your career that may provide insight. The trick with this question is that you must be diplomatic and never bad-mouth your current or previous employer, staff, boss, or customers.

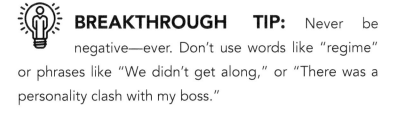 **BREAKTHROUGH TIP:** Never be negative—ever. Don't use words like "regime" or phrases like "We didn't get along," or "There was a personality clash with my boss."

If you're currently employed, the best answer is to say something to the effect of "I'm not 100 percent committed to leaving my current role, and I'm not afraid to say so. The position with your organization represents a stronger opportunity for me and my career. I'm very interested in learning more about your organization and how this might be a great fit for both of us."

If you do not have a job because you were fired or quit after just a couple of months don't lie about your situation—that's unethical. Be transparent and discuss things that were out of your hands, such as company reorganization, downsizing, an acquisition in which positions were eliminated, or the company moved and you were not interested in relocating. If you quit after a few months and you are pressed for details—that can be tricky. Leverage your expertise and what you brought to the previous organization and what you can bring to this new company. Perhaps the role was misrepresented during the interview or the position was downsized. Whatever you say, focus on the positives.

Sometimes, you just have to tell the interviewer that ultimately it wasn't the right fit. "They gave me a couple of options. I decided it would be in everyone's best interest for me to move on and work with a different organization."

This is an exceptionally tricky question, and every situation is different. If you are struggling to come up with a really good explanation, seek consultation from an executive recruiter or reach out to me directly at www.theexecutiveleap.com or 1-844-789-LEAP.

Question #4: Do you have any experience with XYZ?

This is a targeted question, knowingly aimed at something missing from your resume. I refer to this as the "weakness question," because ultimately it is designed to expose just that—your weaknesses.

There are **five key steps to answering a weakness question**, explained by the words: validate, educate, confidence, experience, question. Here's an example.

1. First, *validate* the question by confirming: "I don't have that specific experience with XYZ software."

2. Next, *educate* by explaining: "But I do have experience with QRS software."

3. Then, *show confidence* by saying: "I am confident that I can get up to speed on XYZ software very quickly."

4. After that, demonstrate *experience* by giving an example: "I have gotten up to speed on other similar types of software in the past without any issues."

5. And lastly, *question*, by asking: "Did I give you enough detail?"

Question #5: Why should I hire you?

This is a killer question and one of my favorites because so many candidates are desperately unprepared; they hesitate, they stammer, they ad lib. If that's how you answer, you'll completely blow the interview.

Usually this question comes at the end of an interview, so the best way to answer is to apply what you've learned in the interview. Refer to your notes on your FAB summary, and if you have followed my proven interview strategies (which I'll discuss in chapter 8) you'll have uncovered exactly what the employer wants you to accomplish in the role. Avoid the mistake your competition is going to make by answering the question with a litany of qualifications that really don't tell the interviewer anything new or describe the value you bring to the company and position.

When answering this question, repeat back to the interviewer specifically what the organization is looking for in the role and how you can achieve that for them. Sprinkle in some of your research and finish by telling them, "I can do this for you. That's why you should hire me."

> Let me share with you an example answer to question #5:
> *Wow, that's a great question. Why should you hire me? Let me tell you. In our conversation today, you mentioned that you are looking for somebody to achieve at least a 15 percent reduction in procurement costs over the next twelve to eighteen months. I've done that. In fact, in my current role, I created and implemented a strategy that saved over 35 percent the first year—$47 million. I can do that for you in this position. You indicated a need to centralize procurement into a shared-services organization, and I have done that three times so far in my career. I know what works and what doesn't when it comes to building procurement organizations and can utilize my experiences to help ABC Company. You expressed a concern about leveraging your IT procurement process and building that team. I have done that as well. In addition, your teammates expressed a desire for the new CPO*

to improve stakeholder relationships and eliminate contractors. I have done all of that very successfully throughout my career. Bottom line, my experiences line up quite well with what we have discussed today. I can do this job—I can hit the ground running. Just show me where my office is, the coffee pot and bathrooms, and I will exceed your expectations! That is why you should hire me.

Question #6: Are you overqualified for this position?

The trick with this question is that the interviewer may be concerned that you'll grow dissatisfied with the role and leave. This often occurs if a candidate is interviewing for a role that's something of a step down from a position he or she has held for years, for example, executive vice president, chief operating officer, vice president, or chief operating officer.

The best way to answer this question is to view it as an invitation to teach the interviewer a new way to think about the situation and what you bring to the table. For instance, one answer might be:

I recognize the job market for what it is. It's a marketplace. Like any other marketplace, it's subject to the laws of supply and demand. While you might think I'm overqualified, at the end of the day titles are not important to me. What's important to me is the value that I can bring to your organization. There are very positive benefits for me joining your organization, for both of us at this point.

I work with an executive who has held C-suite roles for the last twenty years. He's ready to take a lesser role—something at the vice-president level—that has less responsibility and less travel. He is running into all kinds of challenges because his resume is covered with C-suite titles, yet he is only interested in vice president roles. He cannot get companies to see past the resume titles and look at the accomplishments and expertise he can bring to the role. For him to be successful in landing his next role, it will be important for him to learn how to answer this question.

Question #7: Where do you see yourself five years from now?

Interviewers ask this question to gauge your level of ambition or see if you're settling for the position, using it as a stepping-stone to get a better job when one comes along, or not really interested in a long-term role.

If you're too specific, you can sound presumptuous. If you're too vague, you're going to come across as rudderless. With your answer, make sure your interviewer knows you are looking for a long-term commitment and that the position entails exactly what you're looking to do. As for your future, you're going to perform to the best of your ability, and whatever future opportunities present themselves, you hope they are with this organization that you're interviewing with.

An example answer to question #7:

I'm definitely interested in making a long-term commitment. Judging by what you shared with me about this role with your company, it's exactly what I'm looking for. I have no doubt I can do this job for you and based on what we discussed, I'm well qualified for the role. As far as my future career path is concerned, I'm confident that this is going to be a long-term commitment between the two of us. I would hope that it would be inevitable that opportunities would present themselves for me to grow within your organization for a long-term fit.

Question #8: You have been with your current company for a long time. Won't it be difficult switching to a new company?

The interviewer is worried that you are stuck in your ways and that the old adage, "It's hard to teach an old dog new tricks," will come into play. The best way to answer this question is to point out the many ways you have grown in your current organization. Highlight the different positions you have held throughout your career with the company, challenges you have faced, your adaptability, and how you thrive on new challenges. To further persuade the interviewer, discuss the similarities of this new role with your current one. Wrap up by assuring the interviewer that you have no doubt that you can do the job since their needs match your skills.

Question #9: What was the toughest part of your last job?

This is a difficult question to answer and is one that can cause problems because the interviewer will assume that whatever you found to be difficult in your current or previous position will translate into your new role. The best way to answer this tricky question is to go for a short close saying, "There was nothing that I found too difficult in my current (or last) role." If that is not enough detail and you are pressed for more information, focus on the most important tasks of the job, explaining how you enjoyed all those—but there were, at times, tasks that were not as important, and how you enjoyed those less.

Question #10: If you were CEO for the day, what would you change?

This question is designed to evaluate your thought process: I have a client who asks every single person she interviews: "If you were CEO for the day, what would you change?" This is a heavy question to ask in an interview, and the way it's asked makes it a trap that can very quickly derail your candidacy.

The best answer to question #10:

> *I would never make a diagnosis within your organization before knowing exactly what the situation is. When you hire me, as I hope you will, I will take a good, hard look at everything your organization is doing, understand why things are being done the way they are, hold some in-depth meetings with you and key people in the organization, and get a good feel of what's being done right and what can be improved.*

Depending on how far you are in the interview, you could name a couple of concerns the interviewer has expressed, and tell him or her that you would start with those and go from there.

Tricky questions are always part of the interviewing process, and knowing how to answer them will position you in the best way possible to leap your competition.

CHAPTER 7 READER TAKEAWAYS:
TRICK-OR-TRAP QUESTIONS

- Be prepared for trick questions.

- Fumbling trap questions can derail your candidacy for a role.

WANT TO KNOW THE ANSWERS THAT HAVE HELPED EXECUTIVES MAKE A 30 PERCENT INCREASE IN COMPENSATION?

CONTACT MIKE AT WWW.THEEXECUTIVELEAP.COM OR GIVE HIM A CALL AT 1-844-789-LEAP FOR INFORMATION ON MORE THAN FORTY TRICK QUESTIONS, INCLUDING HOW TO ANSWER THE SALARY QUESTION

THE INTERVIEW

Test your interview knowledge. Circle *True* or *False*.

1. It is ideal to wing an interview.

    True   *False*

2. The number-one fear of a hiring manager is making a bad hire.

    True   *False*

3. The candidate should ask the first question in an interview.

    True   *False*

4. The person who talks the most in an interview is always the winner.

    True   *False*

5. When answering the "tell me about yourself" question, it's always best to start at the beginning of your career.

    True   *False*

Answers: 1.F; 2.T; 3.T; 4.F; 5.F

By now you have learned that there's a strategy for every step of the process when making an executive leap, positioning yourself as the number-one must-hire, and not settling for the national average of 15 percent increase in compensation.

The interview is the pinnacle of the overall strategy. Without proper preparation, you will fail. Even if you are the best executive in the land, do not think you can wing an interview.

BREAKTHROUGH TIP: Check your ego at the door and follow my breakthrough strategies to ace the interview. Why? According to research conducted by Todd and Jerry, strategic-interview advising does indeed make a significant difference in a candidate's interview success.[23] This research further validates what I have been teaching all these years to my candidates and strategic-advising clients.

Winging an interview is what your competition is doing. Every time an executive has said to me, "Mike, I am good to go. I don't need any interview prep; I have done just fine in my career and will be okay," I've watched him or her blow the interview, ultimately missing out on higher compensation or the job itself.

Most executives have never had interview guidance of any kind. Out of the hundreds of professionals I have worked with on interviewing strategies, fewer than a handful had experienced any previous interview guidance. Now, I am *not* saying you don't know how to interview because, after all, you have been successful in your

---

23 "10 Psychological Techniques to Help You Get a New Job," PSYBLOG, August 24, 2011, http://www.spring.org.uk/2011/08/10-psychological-techniques-to-help-you-get-a-new-job.php.

career so far. However, I *am* saying there are strategies you can employ that help position you as the number-one must-hire candidate, that help you land faster, and that help move you from the average of a 15 percent increase in compensation to well over 30, 40, even 50 percent. Why settle for average?

If you want to make the executive leap, then prepare for your interviews and show up ready to go with my breakthrough interview strategies. These include knowing exactly what the interviewer wants to hear from you (I call this "throwing the first punch" or "getting the questions for the test"), asking meat-on-the-bone thinking questions, listening more than you speak, and knowing where you stand against the competition before closing the interview.

SARA'S STORY

A few years back, we were working on a search for a vice president of indirect procurement for a company in the Midwest. Just as we normally do when working with clients, we talked to a couple hundred professionals before we narrowed down the candidate pool to four who were the best fit, technically and culturally, with the organization. The client chose to start with telephone interviews.

We had conducted strategic-interview guidance with each of the four candidates beforehand. As I do with every professional that I champion into a role, I told each candidate, "I'm not assuming you don't know how to interview. If you were a poor interviewee, you wouldn't be in the executive role you're in now. I'm just giving you strategies to help tighten things up and improve the lay of the land."

One of those four candidates—I'll call her Sara—was superengaging in our pre-interview session prior to her telephone interview. She shared with me that she took multiple pages of notes and practiced per the instructions I gave her. Several days following our session she called to ask some additional questions, so I knew she'd been preparing for her interview, which was scheduled to take place the following day.

She did a great job on the telephone interview and the client reported back to me that they wanted to move her on to the face-to-face interviews. However, in the executive-search business we have a saying, "time kills all deals"—and with this particular client the face-to-face interviews were delayed for a few weeks due to scheduling conflicts (as often happens). Sara, who had been interviewing for multiple roles, was offered another position before my client could get her scheduled for face-to-face interviews. And since "a bird in the hand is worth two in the bush," she took the opportunity that was presented to her. End of story? Not quite.

About three weeks into her new role, the company announced a total reorganization and terminated the person who had hired Sara. A new person was brought in to fill that role and told Sara that he wasn't interested in having her long-term with the organization, and since he hadn't hired her, he felt no sense of loyalty to keep her.

Soon after, she parted ways with that company and called me to ask about the search I had conducted with the first company. As luck would have it, my client's search had been on a temporary hold, so I called my client and explained the situation, and he was absolutely interested in putting Sara back into the mix for a face-to-face interview.

That's how memorable Sara was. And that was from a telephone interview! She had followed the strategies we had put together for a telephone interview that absolutely nailed it for her—to the point that more than a month later she was still memorable.

After I advised Sara through another round of strategic-interviewing sessions, she aced her face-to-face interviews, instantly becoming the company's top choice. A few days later, the client made an unbelievable offer: a more than 30 percent increase in compensation over what Sara had made in her previous position. More than double the national average!

Interview advice armed Sarah with the strategies she could then implement to work her way toward a fantastic position with a great company and a sizeable increase in compensation. Ultimately, it was a perfect match—the client was thrilled and so was Sara. She moved to take the position, and four years later, it is still going great.

THE FACE-TO-FACE INTERVIEW

Hiring managers say they make a hiring decision in the first sixty to ninety seconds.[24] Whether they do or not, as we learned in chapter 6, first impressions do make a difference. Aside from your appearance and handshake, how else can you make a strong first impression?

---

24 "How Interviewers Know When to Hire You in 90 Seconds," Undercover Recruiter, http://theundercoverrecruiter.com/infographic-how-interviewers-know-when-hire-you-90-seconds/.

BREAKTHROUGH TIP: The number-one fear of any hiring manager is making a bad hire.

Ready. Set. Throw the First Punch.

Once you have finished the initial introductions, confirmed the parameters for the interview time, and settled in, it's time to deploy my number-one interview strategy—**throwing the first punch**. Or, in other words, *you ask the first question,* which boils down to: "What are your expectations for this role?" This strategy can be deployed in any interview situation: phone, video, or face-to-face. And it works with a single interviewer or in a group interview.

Throwing the first punch is not an easy way to start an interview, and you will catch people off guard, as it's totally counterintuitive to what normally takes place in an interview. Candidates never ask the first question—but if you do this, you will be rewarded in spades because you will find out exactly what the interviewer wants to hear from you. In essence you are getting the questions to the test and clarity to the interviewer's expectations up front so you can then customize your answers specifically to what they want to hear from you. This is not about fabricating your answers; it's about ensuring that your answers are relevant to the needs and wants of the company and of the people you will interface with in the role. Throwing the first punch is how you set yourself up to eliminate the hiring manager's greatest fear—making a bad hire.

Be a solution to the interviewer's concerns, and you are on your way to making the executive leap. Your competition, on the other hand, is blabbing nonstop about information and achievements in hopes of saying something that the interviewer wants to hear—and failing miserably.

Two Options for Deploying the "First Punch"

Option 1

"It's a pleasure meeting you. Thank you for taking time out of your schedule to meet with me today. Before we get started, I'd appreciate it if you could take a quick minute and tell me what would be expected of me to accomplish in this role?"

Option 2

If meeting with a group: "Hey Joe, John, and Jill, since I will be interfacing with each of you individually in this role, before we get started, would the three of you take a quick minute to tell me one or two things you expect the senior vice president of procurement to accomplish in this role?"

Whether you do this one-on-one with everyone you meet, or in a group interview, I promise each person will provide you at least one expectation that is different from the others. At that point, you can focus on providing accomplishments you have personally achieved that correspond exactly with what your interviewer is looking to hear from you.

By customizing your experience based on what the interviewer or interviewers are looking for, when they are reviewing all the candidates afterward, they'll remember that you specifically addressed their needs—that you were able to match your experience directly to what they said they needed.

Again, as covered in chapter 6 (remember the story of the interviewer that disqualified a fantastic candidate because he arrived without a notepad or portfolio and took zero notes during the interview?), be ready to jot down notes from the answers the interviewers provide. You will refer to these answers throughout the interview by customizing your answers to their specific questions and use them again when closing the interview.

AVOID THE BIGGEST INTERVIEW MISTAKE!

The biggest mistake people make when interviewing (telephone, video, or face-to-face) is talking nonstop about what they think the interviewer wants to hear. The candidate leaves the interview thinking everything went well because he or she talked continuously the entire time. The interviewer, however, has a completely different view of the outcome—essentially that the candidate talked too much! Ever been on a date and the person with you just won't stop talking? Ugh! We've all been there. Don't be the annoying person who just won't shut up. We have two ears and one mouth for a reason. Listen more than you talk. This simple principle is paramount when interviewing.

We had a CIO search, and one of the final candidates was a superstar. He sailed through all the interviews and had one final interview. He was one hour away from a job offer. But hold on, not so fast. At this point, the candidate turned into the annoying date that wouldn't shut up. He literally talked himself right out of a job offer and cost himself several hundred thousand dollars; my client was already discussing salaries that would have been more than a 50 percent increase in total compensation. The hiring manger was extremely disappointed, saying that while the candidate fit the technical aspects of the role perfectly, since he talked so much, he would be a distraction to the team.

Imagine a set of stairs, each step on the staircase is an interview question. Ask my "meat-on-the bone" questions and follow my interview strategies and you will make leaps (take two to three steps at one time) up the staircase and beat the competition to the top. First person to the top wins.

THE EXECUTIVE LEAP'S TOP-TEN QUESTIONS TO ASK THE INTERVIEWER

These meat-on-the-bone questions are designed to help you gain greater insights into the interviewer, the company, and the role, and will be instrumental in helping position you as the number-one must-hire candidate. The interview is a two-way conversation. If you don't engage or ask any questions, it turns into an interrogation. For that reason, you will need to be strategic in asking your questions.

1. **Throw the first punch.** Which, of course, we've already discussed.

2. **"What attracted you to XYZ Widget Company?"** Ideally, you should pose this question directly to a specific interviewer, someone who has been with the company less than two years. Your goal is to find out why someone left a previous position to join this company.

   a. **"What did you find when you joined the company that you didn't expect to find?"**

b. "What were you expecting to find at the company that wasn't here?"

3. **"What are two to three specific projects I'll be working on in the first sixty to ninety days?"** Use "I" in the question to subliminally insert yourself into the role.

4. **"What keeps you coming back day after day?"** This question demonstrates your interest in the interviewer but can help to reveal what an insider (the interviewer) likes best about the company.

5. **"What are three or four characteristics of top performers in your entire organization?"** Ask this directly to everyone you interview with to learn about the desired, leading traits in his or her organization. In essence, you are asking about the corporate culture.

6. **"Tell me about your management style."** Nope—that's what your competition is saying. It's basic, just the bone! Instead, specifically ask the hiring manager: "Joe, tell me about your management style and what characteristics you look for when hiring somebody that's going to produce the most productive working relationship." If you are interviewing with someone who works with Joe, phrase the question this way: "Sally, tell me about Joe's management style. What characteristics does he look for in people that produce great working relationships?"

7. **"What are three to four key contributions you would expect from my performance the first year?"** This is different from the accomplishments question asked when you threw the first punch. In this one, you're ideally looking

for specifics, potentially even some key performance indicators.

8. **"Considering the people in your department or company, can you tell me what your most valued employees are like and what three to five things they do that you believe make them the most successful?"**

9. **"Describe your corporate culture and the type of person who thrives in your organization."** If you've done your homework, you should have some idea of what the culture is like. But getting an insider's view can help you see whether you are truly a best fit.

10. **"Now that you have had time to meet with me and learn about my experiences, how do you see my background adding value to your company?"** This is what's known as a "preclose question," or one to pose near the end of the interview. This question requires the interviewer to verbally provide an answer to your question. So, if positive, they will hear themselves reflect to you why they think you are a good fit. The flip side is it exposes any misunderstandings, what I call yellow lights. If this is the case, there is a way for you to overcome any concerns before the interview is over.

BREAKTHROUGH TIP: Trust your questions. After asking the interviewer a question, don't say another word. Make them provide an answer. You'll need to use the answer at some point later on.

THE EXECUTIVE LEAP'S BREAKTHROUGH STRATEGY FOR INTERVIEW SUCCESS

1. **"Tell me about yourself."** This is often one of the first questions an interviewer asks, and your answer can unnecessarily consume a good portion of the time that's been allotted for the interview. If you've only been in a professional capacity for eight or ten years, it's okay to start with your degree and go from there. If you've been working for twenty or more years, that's too much territory to cover. Either way, ask the interviewer where he or she would like you do start. Often, you'll be asked to start with your current role, or they'll select a point in your resume and ask you to start with that. Note: when talking about your career history, make sure to sprinkle in the accomplishments and benefits you can bring to the company. (Refer to your FAB summary.)

2. **Never fabricate.** While you want to be able to customize your answers based on what the interviewers are looking for, you must never fabricate an answer.

3. **"I can do this for you."** Once or twice per half hour, remind the interviewers that you're the person for the job with a statement such as, "I can do this for you."

    As I mentioned earlier in this book, everyone you're going to interview with is busy; they're all overworked, they were asked last minute to meet with you, and often they're in the dark about you—having not even seen your resume. They're in a hurry to get through the interview, and maybe only 70 percent of their attention is actually focused on what's going on in the room. The rest of their mind is thinking about what else they have to get done that day and the fires they still have to put out.

If you remind them several times that you've done this work—*you can do this for them*—they're going to write in their notes "Candidate can do this, can do that." Then later, when the interviews are over and the hiring

> **With your repeated statement "I can do this," you're subliminally poking the interviewer to choose you when the time comes.**

manager is asking opinions, the interviewers will recall from their notes: "Candidate said he/she can do this." With your repeated statement "I can do this," you're subliminally poking the interviewer to choose you when the time comes.

4. **Be succinct.** Remember, we have two ears and one mouth for a reason. That's the advice I tell executives during our strategic interview-readiness process. People that talk the most in a conversation are the ones who typically think the conversation was fantastic.

So skip the minutia, the less-than-important details, when answering questions. For example, if the question is "Tell me about a time you improved a process for your organization," your answer might be, "Great question. In fact, I've done that numerous times throughout my career. One specifically was when I was with XYZ

Widget Company. We were taking forty-five days to do a month-end close. I was able to implement a close strategy that knocked fifteen days off that close. It worked out great and was implemented company wide."

When you're finished answering the question succinctly, ask the interviewer if he or she wants you to elaborate, and then do so if requested. Ask one of the following: "Did I give you enough detail? Would you like me to drill down further? Was I clear on that?" Let the interviewer tell you when he or she needs to know more. Regardless of whom you're interviewing with, listen more than you talk; be informative but succinct with your answers.

5. **Collect business cards.** If you haven't collected them already, get business cards from the interviewers before you leave. In the next chapter, I'll talk about how to reach out after the interview, and those business cards will give you the information you need to connect with your interviewers. In chapter 6, I mentioned having business cards made, and here's why: handing people your business card is a great way of getting their card in return.

6. **Benefits?** Don't inquire about benefits unless the interviewer brings them up. Benefits are important, but you will get to those when an offer is made. In fact, don't bring them up at all. If you are presented to a company by an executive recruiter, they should already have a good idea of how your current benefits match up with what the client offers.

7. **Compensation?** The compensation question—how much are you looking for—usually doesn't come up in the face-to-face interview with hiring managers who are well prepared. If it does come up, do not answer with a dollar figure. And never tell an interviewer that you're currently underpaid; no company wants to hear that you think you're working below market value—even though that is not uncommon in a postrecession era when people took jobs with dramatic salary cuts.

> For more strategies on how to answer the compensation question, visit www.theexecutiveleap.com, or contact Mike Sudermann at 1-844-789-LEAP.

EVERY INTERVIEW COUNTS

Often, after a candidate has gone through several interviews, there's one last interview with a senior member of the organization. This is usually someone the candidate won't ultimately report to, but it's a senior-level person who must give the final thumbs-up before the hire is confirmed. Even for chief executive officers, the board of directors must all approve the hire.

Early in my career, I was placing a candidate for a controller with a major soft-drink manufacturer. He was a shoe-in, and he knew it. He made it through all the interviews and then was called in for one last interview with the EVP of finance—someone who this role didn't report to but who influenced the final hiring decision. I guided the candidate on tone and a few other last needs for the interview including, "Check your ego at the door."

When he arrived at the interview (late, no less), he was disheveled and completely unprepared, stumbling over his words and rambling on with his answers. In short, he blew it.

In the debriefing, the hiring manager conveyed to me the EVP's assessment: no way would the company hire this candidate. He wasn't the right fit, talked too much, came across as cocky, and didn't listen. It was a lousy situation all around.

You must be on your game with every single interview, no matter whom you're talking to. Even if you've been interviewing for three weeks straight and you're told that this one last interview is just a matter of principle, you still have to bring your best game, dress the part, and come *prepared* to interview with that person, because he or she is going to have some level of influence on the ultimate decision. Period.

You're going up against other superstars when it comes to landing a new role—so show up to win, not just to play. Utilize my proven breakthrough strategies to ensure success.

CLOSING THE INTERVIEW

To close on a high note, ask a preclosing question that reveals where you stand in the interview process at that point in time. Question #10 from page 129 ("Now that you have had time to meet with me and learn about my experiences, how do you see my background adding value to your company?") is a solid preclosing question. Your interviewer's answer determines your next steps.

BREAKTHROUGH TIP: One of the biggest mistakes made when interviewing is not asking for the job. I suggest you ask subliminally using the preclose statement . . .

After you finish with Question #10, begin closing the interview on your end. If you are genuinely interested in the role, start closing by making the following statement: "Jim, thanks again for your time today. Based on our conversation, coupled with speaking to Steve, Sally, Emily, and Jeff, I have no doubt I can hit the ground running and do this job for you. I am very interested in the role and would like to know—what are the next steps?"

When interviewing with multiple people, the second person you interview with is your starting point. Tie in the first person's interview in the closing with the second interview and so on. For example: "Sally, based on my conversation with you today and with Steve, I am very excited about this position, and based on what I know so far, I have no doubt I can do this job for you and XYZ Widget Company."

BREAKTHROUGH TIP: At this late stage, avoid the word "opportunity." Now that you've made it this far, the position is not an opportunity anymore; the interview was the opportunity—now you're talking about the *position*.

IT'S A PROCESS

Bottom line: The job search for executives is a process, and you must go through it every time if you want to make the leap. The following story is an example of what happens when the process *isn't* followed completely.

COLLIN'S STORY

I found a candidate who was a terrific fit for a role; in fact, it was pretty much a no-brainer. I championed him into my client and strategically prepped him for the interview. He knew all the players, and he was such a great fit in experience, salary range, and culture that he could hit the ground running and there'd be no looking back on anyone's part. This was early in my career, so I was really happy that he was so excited and that I'd made such a good match.

But during the post-interview debriefing with the candidate, I knew something had gone terribly wrong because all he talked about was how great it was to meet up with an old friend. It turned out that the interviewer had been a classmate of the candidate from high school, and instead of going through all the steps I'd guided him through, he and the interviewer sat there for an hour talking about the good old days. Very little of the conversation had actually been an interview of the candidate for the role.

"Did you ask the opening question?" I asked him.

"Well, no," he replied, "because we started talking about old times."

"Did you ask the closing question?"

"Well, not really, because he had already told me he was excited to see me, that he already knew me, and that this is a really fortunate situation."

"What did you talk about?"

"Well, I asked a few questions when we talked, but he said that he felt pretty good about everything. So I'm excited about it."

That was the candidate's debriefing statement.

It turned out that my fears were confirmed. The client told me that he knew the candidate twenty years ago, but in the interview, he'd barely been able to get a word in edgewise. "He's not going to be the right fit for what we need," the client told me.

The moral of this story: Even if you're interviewing with your second cousin or a neighbor you knew ten years ago, *go through the process*. There's a method to the madness, a reason I've put this process together—because it works! A hiring manager's number-one fear is making a bad hire, and yet interviewers will often decide on candidates within the first couple minutes of meeting them.

In this instance, the candidate could have—and should have—knocked the interview out of the park. And that twenty-year bond may have given him an edge over other, equally qualified candidates. Instead, he bypassed the process and didn't make it beyond the first face-to-face interview.

CHAPTER 8 READER TAKEAWAYS:
THE INTERVIEW

- Don't wing it.

- Be ready to be memorable.

- Throw the first punch; this is about getting the questions to the test so that you can tailor your answers throughout the interview.

- Preparation is the core of a winning interview strategy.

- Being memorable in a positive way is critical to interview success.

- Don't talk nonstop! Be concise with answers, and then ask if more clarity is needed.

- Be ready to talk about your experience, but maximize the time you have available.

- Remember: Every interview counts!

- Remember: The interview is a two-way conversation!

- Be prepared to ask your own questions of the interviewers. Sample questions include:

  - What attracted you to XYZ Widget Company?

  - What keeps you coming back day after day?

  - What are three or four characteristics of top performers in your company?

- Begin closing the interview with the question: "Now that you have had time to meet with me, how do you see my background adding value to your company?"

- Never fabricate.

- Repeat this statement often: "I can do this for you."

- Collect business cards from the interviewers.

GO TO WWW.THEEXECUTIVELEAP.COM FOR MORE INFORMATION ON COMPENSATION DISCUSSIONS

C H A P T E R   9

POST INTERVIEW

Test your post-interview knowledge. Circle *True* or *False*.

1. It's okay to send a thank-you email within three business days.

    True   *False*

2. Ideally a thank-you email should explain in detail your interview conversation.

    True   *False*

3. Handwritten thank-you notes are considered outdated and unnecessary.

    True   *False*

4. The fancier the thank-you note, the better.

    True   *False*

5. Once receiving an offer, take a week to make your decision.

    True   *False*

In the executive-search business, we say time kills all deals. It's no different for candidates interviewing. Time will kill your opportunity with a company quickly if you do not have a post-interview strategy for sending thank-you notes and accepting offers.

Send thank-you notes to the interviewers you met with immediately following the interview. To leap your competition, it's imperative that you send these notes in a timely manner. Robert learned that lesson the hard way.

ROBERT'S STORY

Robert interviewed for a vice president of sales role and did not send a single thank-you e-mail or handwritten note for three days. He was invited back for a final interview and told that if he hadn't done such a great job interviewing, he would have been passed up for a final interview because he didn't send a thank-you note in a timely manner. Time kills all deals.

THE E-MAIL THANK-YOU

E-mail thank-you notes are expected after interview, ideally within three to four *hours* and no later than the end of the day. In the subject line of the e-mail, include the title of the position you interviewed for. For example: "The director of sales interview today" or "Jeff Smith, director of sales candidate."

Write the e-mail much like you would a letter. For instance:

Hello Jill,

I hope this e-mail finds you well.

Thank you for taking time to meet with me today to discuss the director of sales role with XYZ Widget Company.

I truly enjoyed our conversation, especially [insert something specific you discussed with Jill].

As I shared with you, I have no doubt I can hit the ground running and achieve your sales goals.

I look forward to the next steps of the process.

Sincerely,

[Full Name]

The key to the e-mail is to tailor it to the recipient. Base your specific details on something from your conversation with that individual. This is where your meat-on-the-bone questions and the notes you took will come in handy.

Don't write an overly long thank-you note. Keep it short. Don't wax philosophical about how great you are and why they would be fools not to hire you. Don't include six paragraphs and a bulleted list of what you bring to the table—that makes you sound desperate. I've actually had clients disqualify candidates who wrote superlong thank-you notes or notes with poor grammar or misspelled words. Spell-check the e-mail and check it visually before clicking send.

EXAMPLE OF AN E-MAIL THANK-YOU NOTE THAT'S TOO LONG

Dear Courtney:

Thank you for taking the time to talk with me today about the opportunity at XXX. I am very excited about this role and

I have no doubt that I could lead a procurement transformation in partnership with you.

My last four roles have been helping businesses transform their operations and making the cultural journey toward establishing a center of procurement excellence. I can help you in the following areas we discussed.

- *Savings—returning savings in categories of spend and putting it on XXX bottom line.*

- *Partnership—developing strong working relationships with functional areas (like IT) and helping them with contracting processes. This would shine a light on these activities so you will be comfortable that they proceed with a high level of transparency.*

- *Culture—Your transformation will require a leader that can positively influence culture by (i) leading with the vision, (ii) making decisions with wisdom, strength and grace, (iii) empowering teams within boundaries, and (iv) living the company's values.*

This journey will be difficult (but fun!), and I have spearheaded these transformations multiple times and have the deep experience a leader needs to create success for your team.

If you have any questions about my experience or capabilities, or if you find that you need some advice about procurement questions, please call me at any time at 703-XXX-XXXX.

My warmest regards,

[Full Name]

THE HANDWRITTEN THANK-YOU

Ideally, the same day you interview, send a short, handwritten thank-you note. This is where having the interviewer's business card will be especially handy. If you just wrapped up a face-to-face interview, find a coffee shop nearby, write out your thank-you notes, then return back to the company and give them to the receptionist. If it's after hours, drop them into a mailbox.

I recommend using stationery cards; they don't have to say "thank you" on the cover, but they can. Don't go overboard with your choice of cards; they can have your name inscribed on them, but keep the look professional, corporate.

The verbiage on the handwritten card is a little different from the e-mail:

Sally,

Thanks so much for taking time to interview with me for the director of sales position on Tuesday, March 1, 2016.

I truly enjoyed our conversation, especially discussing strategy for the franchise rollout. As expressed, I'm very interested in the role.

I look forward to meeting with you again soon.

Best regards,

[Full Name]

That's it—and here's why: People rarely get handwritten thank-you notes anymore. And the fact that you took the time and had the initiative to put one together—and dropped back by the receptionist at the company or popped it in the mail the same day— will make a huge statement, a lasting impression on the interviewer.

I know candidates who have gotten jobs because of handwritten thank-you notes.

If you've flown in for the interview, bring your own cards and envelopes with you. Don't forget stamps or prestamp your envelopes. While you're waiting for your flight back, write your thank-you notes and drop them in the mailbox at the airport. The key is to get the cards in the mail before you leave town.

YOU RECEIVED AN OFFER!

Congratulations! By this time you have no doubt spent the last two to three months traveling and interviewing with the company. At this point, I strategically advise my executives to accept verbally within twenty-four hours if at all possible. The time frame can vary due to the seniority of the role and complexity of the offer, but most companies start getting antsy as the days start adding up.

Quite frankly, after two or three months of interviewing, you should be able to provide a verbal answer in no more than forty-eight hours. The idea of taking a week to think about your answer seems like a stalling technique to companies. Do you want the job or not? In all my years of extending offers, most executives who have not accepted verbally within twenty-four to forty-eight hours end up not taking the job. Time kills all deals.

When it comes to an offer letter, an executive recruiter can help clear the air by exposing factors in the equation that you may not have considered. For instance, I had a candidate in New York reach out to me for advice on taking a president/CEO role in California. It was a terrific opportunity, but it had what I call substantial "flies in ointment"—it was a messy and very complicated offer. We discussed the role, location, company culture, and many other points of consideration at length—and ultimately he passed on the offer.

THE VALUE OF A STRATEGIC-SEARCH ADVISOR

While I've shared with you throughout the book a number of tips for helping you in your endeavor to land a new role, I cannot overstate the value of first-hand guidance from an executive strategic-search advisor.

Preparation strategies absolutely help professionals make the executive leap, especially when it comes to leveraging you as the number-one must-hire to land your next job and receive the highest-possible compensation. Here's one of my favorite success stories.

STEVE'S STORY

A private-equity firm hired us to conduct a senior-level search. Ultimately three people would shake out for the face-to-face interviews, but in the very beginning there were only two individuals—we'll call them Joe and Jeff—that the client was really sold on. It was a "flip-the-coin" kind of scenario.

Then a late submittal entered the race. "Steve," we'll call him, had less experience than the other two but met the client's must-haves so we presented him. The client agreed to interview him, although they were not expecting much to come of it. They just wanted to make sure all the bases were covered.

We strategically prepped all three candidates, and of the three, Steve asked the most questions. He phoned me, texted me, followed up on the guidelines, and we even did some role-playing.

Now, what makes this particular story interesting is that the client told Joe that he would make a great fit for the organization. The company did not make a formal offer, but in the interview they asked, "If we make you an offer, when can you start?" So while Joe didn't quit his job, he had begun coordinating schedules and making plans with his family to move to take on this new position.

Then Steve went to an in-person interview, which the client essentially thought was obligatory. Again, the client was just kind of going through the motions to be sure they covered all the bases. The interview took place at three o'clock on a Friday afternoon—and Steve nailed it. He did a phenomenal job.

After the interview, I circled back with the client and heard them gush over Steve, saying he exceeded their expectations and that they had already received thank-you notes. I was happy to hear Steve had followed my advice. In less than four hours, the client had decided to make Steve the offer instead of Joe. At seven o'clock on a Friday night, the client was preparing an offer to make over the weekend because they didn't want to let Steve get away.

The offer took Steve from a director to a senior vice president position and brought him a more than $225,000 increase in compensation. (He accepted, of course.)

CHAPTER 9 READER TAKEAWAYS:
THE POST INTERVIEW

- Time kills all deals. Have a post-interview strategy.

- Send a thank-you e-mail within three to four hours following the interview.

- Be concise when thanking the interviewer.

- Base the content of your e-mailed thank-you note on details from the conversation in the interview.

- Handwritten thank-you notes make a huge impact. Send a short, handwritten note the same day as the interview.

- Scrutinize all thank-you notes for spelling as closely as you do your resume, whether the note is e-mailed or handwritten.

VISIT WWW.THEEXECUTIVELAP.COM TO LEARN MORE ABOUT INTERVIEW PREPARATION STRATEGIES OR CALL MIKE AT 1-844-789-LEAP TO DISCUSS INTERVIEW PREP OR OFFER RESPONSES

CONCLUSION

By now, I hope you understand what it's going to take to make the executive leap. My breakthrough strategies covered how to leverage your resume, cover letter, social media, interview, and post interview to land your next top job. To top it off, you learned the value of a strategic-search advisor like me, who can help position you as the number-one must-hire to land your next top job without settling for less-than-average compensation.

"THE QUESTION"

No, I'm not talking about popping *the* question. But remember the last time you posed an idea to your significant other—maybe a home-improvement project, teaching the kids a new skill, or planning a vacation? Did he or she just nod and give the idea lip service, agreeing to show up and go along for the ride, or just telling you "I got this" and then, basically, dropping the ball? Or did he or she get excited, get involved, and then—with the two of you working together—reach a great outcome?

It's the same with the strategic-search advisor / executive relationship. The real value in guidance occurs when you, the executive, are a willing participant in the process of making the leap.

To demonstrate, let me tell you a final story about a search that occurred a few years ago, when a client hired us to find the company a vice president of finance.

GEORGE'S STORY

George was a finance executive that was ready to make a career move. We worked together to get him presented to a client, who invited him to interview. As a candidate, I advised him through the telephone interview, and he moved on to the face-to-face.

During the interview, George had a lengthy conversation with Dennis, the chief operating officer. As part of his prep work, George knew that prior to the final wrap-up, he needed to close the interview with a question such as, "Thank you so much for taking time to meet with me today. Now that we've had this long conversation, how do you see me adding value to your organization?" Then, as he'd been advised, he stopped and didn't say another word.

However, the reply to his question was entirely unex-pected. "I'm not really sure how you would add value," the COO said.

Although George was at first taken aback, he remained composed and proceeded to boil down what had been a ninety-minute conversation into a less-than-five-minute summary of his previous answers to demonstrate the value he would bring to the table. Then he repeated his question: "How do you see me adding value to your organization?"

This time, the COO answered, "Now I get it. I think you'd be a great fit. We need to bring you in for one more round of face-to-face interviews."

Ultimately, George ended up getting the job. But if he hadn't had the strategic advice—and followed it—he would have been one of the 95 percent of people who just show up and regurgitate their resume during the interview process. He very likely wouldn't have known that what was needed to alleviate confusion at the close of the interview was to *reinforce his value*.

BREAKTHROUGH TIP: Today, it's no longer enough to be a superstar and show up with a dazzling smile and dressed to the nines, resume in hand. Today, you must employ breakthrough strategies if you're going to make the executive leap.

I'm available anytime, by any means, to continue answering questions and sharing my proven breakthrough strategies to prepare you to make the executive leap. As an executive looking to make a job change, you have a considerable amount of work ahead of you. But by following my breakthrough strategies to make an otherwise-frustrating process unbelievably straightforward, you will avoid common pitfalls and mishaps made by even the most seasoned professionals. The strategies I've laid out are easy to follow, proven, and aimed at you, the mid- to senior-level executive looking for the right career move *without settling*. As your strategic-search advisor, I know the ins and outs of the executive marketplace. I help you understand the salary ranges for specific roles, the opportunities for your industry or functional niche, your position within the marketplace, and the time it will take you to land.

But still, in the end, it really is a process of, to recoin an old phrase, "leading a horse to water." I can lead you there, and I can show you what to do, but it's up to *you* to drink once you're there. Fortunately, that's what George did, and it landed him a phenomenal role.

So the question is: **Are *you* ready to make the executive leap?**

A P P E N D I X   A

LinkedIn Privacy-
Setting Adjustment

With LinkedIn, you have a variety of privacy settings. When making changes to your profile, I recommend you spare your connections from receiving an announcement each and every time you update your profile. Turn off announcements or adjust privacy settings by following these steps:

- Go to your profile, click your picture in the upper right-hand corner of the screen, click **Privacy & Settings** in the drop-down that displays.

- On your Account page, select the **Privacy** tab.

- Select **Sharing profile edits**, and select **No**. This action will turn off sharing so that your connections are not notified every time you make a change to your profile.

- Once you are satisfied with our updates, turn the notifications back on.

Keywords and Keyword Phrases for your Resume and Social Media Profiles

Do you know which keywords and key phrases are best for your functional niche? I can help you sort out the best words to include in your resume and online.

SAMPLE KEYWORDS

Make sure to use your industry-specific words.

- budgeting
- leadership
- benchmarking
- influenced
- overhauled
- diversified
- enhanced
- maximized
- valued
- promoted
- obtained
- facilitated
- generated
- improved
- published
- conducted

- modernized
- strengthened
- restructured
- upgraded
- validated
- reengineered
- reorganized
- distinguished
- unified
- launched
- partnered
- innovative
- administered
- safeguarded
- negotiated
- headed
- quantified
- accomplished
- delivered
- achieved
- earned
- managed
- entrepreneurial
- facilitated
- analyzed
- monitored
- oversaw
- streamlined
- transformed
- forecasting
- implemented
- redesigned
- turnaround
- versatile
- dynamic
- global
- international
- adaptable

SAMPLE KEYWORD PHRASES

- crisis management
- best practices
- multisite operations
- world-class operations
- profit and loss (P&L)
- new business development
- strategic leadership
- client relationships
- continuous improvement
- trusted advisor
- product management
- technology development
- digital imaging
- portfolio management

- profitability improvement
- performance optimization
- corporate administration
- process mapping
- risk mitigation
- project management
- cross functional
- strategic thinker
- change management
- succession planning
- technical due diligence
- sample processing
- value engineering
- construction management
- product development
- sales optimization

Make sure you include all your skills—even the ones you may not be using—in your current role. This is a big mistake people make that oftentimes gets them passed up on opportunities. Be sure to include the following:

- industry professional or technical acronyms;

- relevant industry and professional organizations;

- awards, honors, and recognition;

- job-specific or industry-specific software, hardware that is relevant to your profession; and

- licenses, patents, publications, and major projects.

FAB© Worksheet Sample

To separate yourself from other candidates you must go into interviews extremely well prepared. The best thing you can do is *not* regurgitate what is already on your resume.

We suggest you complete our FAB Sheet (feature / accomplishment / benefits). The FAB Sheet is a comprehensive inventory of your specific career accomplishments that will help you prepare for any interview.

First, it shows specifically what you can do for the employer- how you will benefit him or her and the organization. Secondly, it details what you have accomplished in your current and previous positions, and lastly, it highlights your unique features and experiences.

Let's define terms: **features** are facts about you, **accomplishments** are significant measurable results (stated in numbers, fractions, dollars, or percentages) that you obtained for your current or past employers and **benefits** are educated guesses of what you can do for a new employer based on your accomplishments.

HOW TO PREPARE A FAB WORKSHEET

1. Set aside several hours.

2. Analyze each position you have held and what you have accomplished.

3. List features highlighting your education, number of years in the industry, and various experiences, patents, licenses, awards, special seminars, and unique life experiences.

4. In chronological order from present to past, prepare a timetable of your employment history. Under features, list all positions and significant duties no matter how small, including all promotions. List all accomplishments for each position. Try to quantify them with specific accomplishments using numerical percentages and/or volumes wherever possible. Employers want to see (1) WHAT you accomplished and (2) HOW you accomplished it. The accomplishment section is extremely critical in quantifying how you accomplished what you have accomplished. Then identify your specific talents and how you can benefit the new employer because of your past experiences, accomplishments, and training. Choose the most compelling reasons someone should hire you in preference to someone else and how your past accomplishments would make you head and shoulders above someone else.

FAB SET-UP WORKSHEET

FEATURES	ACCOMPLISHMENTS	BENEFITS TO EMPLOYER
Facts about you.	Significant measurable results obtained for your current or past employers. Money saved, money made, and processes improved.	Educated guesses of what you can do for a new employer based on your features and accomplishments.

FAB SUMMARY OF PROFESSIONAL EXPERIENCES AND ACCOMPLISHMENTS

POSITION	TOP 3-4 RESPONSIBILITIES	KEY QUANTIFIABLE ACCOMPLISHMENTS	BENEFITS TO EMPLOYER
CABELA'S VP GM – Retail Merchandising	1) GM General Merchandising 2) Hired to restructure merch and inventory organization 3) Innovated retail merch process 4) Developed & implemented e-Comm footwear strategy	1) $10 M increase in footwear sales first 18 months of implementing new strategy 2) Created $100 M footwear partnership 3) 16% increase in boot sales 4) Received Chairman's award for outstanding improvement of a particular category.	1) Turnaround Specialist 2) Footwear expert 3) Build or substantially improve brand / category identity 4) Build strategic partnerships that result in revenue growth
HARRY AND DAVID SVP Retail Stores and Wholesale Division	1) Hired to substantially improve brand identity 2) Lead innovation to grow business and reduce 3) Increase sales	1) $5 M annual increase in sales by leading and implementing a new merchandising model 2) $50 M multi-year strategic partnership established that increased sales while reducing costs by leveraging packaging and distribution costs	1) Highly networked and able to build strategic partnerships resulting in revenue growth 2) Innovative 3) Highly experienced retail sales executive in branding, merchandising, strategy, innovation, and marketing.
NIKE GM, Retail	1) Hired to manage exclusive collection, merchandise procurement, retail marketing, and field operations for 17 Niketown locations and Nike.com 2) Increase revenues 3) Reduce costs	1) 800 Basis point improvement in turn up 1.2 from previous year 2) 29% increase in SKU productivity 3) 19% ROI on store marketing events 4) Rewrote all store training programs to include awards program built customer relationship loyalty software program SOPs	1) Increase efficiencies of retail store operations 2) Innovative marketing ideas 3) Build customer loyalty programs
LIZ CLAIBORNE VP Marketing & Sales	1) Hired to improve marketing across all departments 2) Direct merchandise development 3) Manage field sales teams and distribution across US merchandisers across the US	1) $73 M increase in sales growth in three years 2) 300% increase in store revenues	1) Establish strong partnerships with senior merchants 2) Direct merchandise development of all fashion / apparel products 3) Manage and grow sales & merchandisers teams 4) Strong store / product distribution knowledge

NOTES:

FOR THE QUESTIONS YOU NEED TO BEST COMPLETE YOUR FAB WORKSHEET, VISIT WWW.THEEXECUTIVELEAP.COM

Word Counts for Your LinkedIn Profile

- first name: 20 characters, last name: 40 characters

- professional headline: 120 character limit

- summary: 2,000 character limit

- recommendation: 3,000 character limit

- LinkedIn publisher post headline: 100 maximum characters

- LinkedIn publisher post body: 40,000 characters

- website anchor text: 30 maximum characters

- website URL: 256 maximum characters

- vanity URL: 29 characters after "www.linkedin.com/in/"

- position title: 100 character limit

- position description: 200 minimum and 2,000 max

- interests: 1,000 character limit

- additional info / advice for contacting: 2,000 character limit

- phone number: 25 character limit

- IM (instant message): 25 character limit

- address: 1,000 character limit

- skills: 80 characters per skill

- company name: 100 maximum characters

- company page description: 200 min / 1,500 max

- company page specialties: 256 maximum characters

- company update: 600 characters, or 250 if including a link

- showcase page name: 100 maximum characters

- showcase page description: 75 min / 200 max

- LinkedIn status update: 600 maximum characters

- LinkedIn message (InMail): 2,000 character limit

- group discussion title: 200 maximum characters

- group discussion body: 2,000 characters

- group discussion comments: 1,000 characters

- LinkedIn text ad headline: 25 character limit

- LinkedIn text ad message body: 75 character limit

- LinkedIn direct sponsored content: 160 character limit

- profile "publication" title: 255 characters

- profile "publication" description: 2,000 characters[25]

---

25   Andy Foote, "Maximum LinkedIn Character Counts for 2016," https://www. linkedin.com/pulse/maximum-linkedin-character-counts-2016-andy-foote.

A P P E N D I X   E

Pre-Interview Checklist

✓ **Appearance**

You only have a few seconds to make a great first impression and how you dress for the interview is a common way talent is initially assessed. Are you a serious candidate and will you fit culturally are evaluated almost immediately by dress. Men, dress conservatively: white or blue shirt, dark suit. Shine shoes, shave, and don't use cologne. Women should wear a dark business suit; avoid crazy distracting jewelry, earrings, and fingernail polish. No perfume.

✓ **Confirm Date, Time, and Location**

Make sure you get all logistics covered: address of the company, directions, company phone number, where to park, and who to ask for upon arrival. If air travel is required, confirm hotel (if applicable). Plan on arriving and being in the building ten to fifteen minutes early just in case you run into traffic issues or the company asks you to complete paperwork.

✓ **Multiple Copies of Your Resume**

Bring three to four copies of your resume. Sometimes people are asked to participate in the interview not originally scheduled or the interviewer has not seen your resume.

✓ **References**

List your references on a separate document and bring multiple copies with you to the interview.

✓ **List of Questions**

Bring a prepared list of questions for each person you are going to meet. This enables you to keep separate notes for each person that interviews you.

✓ **FAB Summary**

Make sure you have this information handy for reference purposes regardless of the type of interview. There is additional space on summary to keep notes.

✓ **Portfolio Including a Pad of Paper and Several Pens**

Bring the portfolio to hold extra copies of references, resumes, and prepared questions.

✓ **Snack, Medications, and Water**

Treat an interview like an athletic event. Just in case the interview(s) go long you want to make sure you have a quick snack available. I suggest a protein bar that has a good ratio of carbohydrates, protein, and fat for energy. Bring any needed medications and a bottle of water.

✓ **Business Cards (if applicable)**

Always bring four to five current business cards. If unemployed, I suggest creating your own business card using executive level card stock with your name and contact information on front and your FAB on the back. While some executive candidates will have business cards, not all will have a business card with their FAB on the back, and that is a huge differentiation.

✓ **Thank-You Note Cards, Envelopes, and Stamps (if applicable)** Bring four to five note cards with you to write a short thank-you note to each person you interviewed. Go to a local coffee shop and write your notes, keeping them short and simple. Hand-deliver to the receptionist or drop in the mailbox. I have done this many times in my career with great success. You will definitely make an excellent impression.

A P P E N D I X   F

Income Tax Bracket Considerations

Before accepting a job offer that involves moving out of state, it is important you have a good handle on what your new state income tax bracket will be. Especially if you are moving out of a "no income tax state" such as Florida, Texas, South Dakota, or others noted here. Being armed with the proper information is valuable when negotiating your compensation package.

	Single Filer			Married - Filing Jointly		
State	Rates		Income	Rates		Income
Alabama	5.00%	>	$3,000	5.00%	>	$6,000
Alaska	No State Income Tax			No State Income Tax		
Arizona	4.24%	>	$50,000	4.24%	>	$100,000
	4.54%	>	$150,000	4.54%	>	$300,000
Arkansas	6.90%	>	$35,099	6.90%	>	$35,099
California	9.30%	>	$51,530	9.30%	>	$103,060
	10.30%	>	$263,222	10.30%	>	$526,444

	11.30%	>	$315,866	11.30%	>	$631,732
	12.30%	>	$526,443	12.30%	>	$1,000,000
	13.30%	>	$1,000,000	13.30%	>	$1,052,886
Colorado	4.63% of federal taxable income			4.63% of federal taxable income		
Connecti-cut	6.00%	>	$100,000	6.00%	>	$200,000
	6.50%	>	$200,000	6.50%	>	$400,000
	6.90%	>	$250,000	6.90%	>	$500,000
	6.99%	>	$500,000	6.99%	>	$1,000,000
Delaware	6.60%	>	$60,000	6.60%	>	$60,000
Florida	No State Income Tax			No State Income Tax		
Georgia	6.00%	>	$7,000	6.00%	>	$10,000
Hawaii	8.25%	>	$48,000	8.25%	>	$96,000
Idaho	7.40%	>	$10,890	7.40%	>	$21,780
Illinois	3.75% of federal taxable income			3.75% of federal taxable income		
Indiana	3.3% of federal taxable income			3.3% of federal taxable income		
Iowa	8.98%	>	$69,930	8.98%	>	$69,930
Kansas	4.60%	>	$15,000	4.60%	>	$30,000
Kentucky	6.00%	>	$75,000	6.00%	>	$75,000

Louisiana	6.00%	>	$50,000	6.00%	>	$100,000
Maine	7.15%	>	$37,499	7.15%	>	$74,999
Maryland	5.00%	>	$100,000	5.00%	>	$150,000
	5.25%	>	$125,000	5.25%	>	$175,000
	5.50%	>	$150,000	5.50%	>	$225,000
	5.75%	>	$250,000	5.75%	>	$300,000
Massachu-setts	5.10%	>	$0	5.10%	>	$0
Michigan	4.25% of federal AGI with modification			4.25% of federal AGI with modification		
Minnesota	7.85%	>	$82,740	7.85%	>	$146,270
	9.85%	>	$155,650	9.85%	>	$259,420
Mississippi	5.00%	>	$10,000	5.00%	>	$10,000
Missouri	6.00%	>	$9,000	6.00%	>	$9,000
Montana	6.90%	>	$17,400	6.90%	>	$17,400
Nebraska	6.84%	>	$29,590	6.84%	>	$59,180
Nevada	No State Income Tax			No State Income Tax		
New Hampshire	5.00%	>	$0	5.00%	>	$0
New Jersey				5.525%	>	$80,000
	6.37%	>	$75,000	6.37%	>	$150,000
	8.97%	>	$500,000	8.97%	>	$500,000

New Mexico	4.90%	>	$16,000	4.90%	>	$24,000
New York	6.65%	>	$80,150	6.65%	>	$160,500
	6.85%	>	$214,000	6.85%	>	$321,050
	8.82%	>	$1,070,350	8.82%	>	$2,140,900
North Carolina	5.75%	>	$0	5.75%	>	$0
North Dakota	2.27%	>	$90,750	2.27%	>	$151,200
	2.64%	>	$189,300	2.64%	>	$230,450
	2.90%	>	$411,500	2.90%	>	$411,500
Ohio	3.960%	>	$83,350	3.960%	>	$83,350
	4.597%	>	$104,250	4.597%	>	$104,250
	4.997%	>	$208,500	4.997%	>	$208,500
Oklahoma	5.00%	>	$7,200	5.00%	>	$12,200
Oregon	9.90%	>	$125,000	9.90%	>	$250,000
Pennsylvania	3.07%	>	$0	3.07%	>	$0
Rhode Island	4.75%	>	$60,850	4.75%	>	$60,850
	5.99%	>	$138,300	5.99%	>	$138,300
South Carolina	7.00%	>	$14,600	7.00%	>	$14,600
South Dakota	No State income Tax			No State Income Tax		

Tennessee	0%	>	$0	0%	>	$0

No Income Tax on Salaries and Wages

As of April 2016, TN fully eliminated personal income tax. However, investment income has a six-year phase in and will be subject to tax until 2022. http://www.nathaniel-jacobson.com/single-post/2016/07/26/Tennessee-To-Become-the-Eighth-NoIncome-Tax-State

Texas	No State Income Tax			No State Income Tax		
Utah	5.00%	>	$0	5.00%	>	$0
Vermont	7.80%	>	$93,400	7.80%	>	$160,450
	8.80%	>	$192,400	8.80%	>	$240,000
	8.95%	>	$415,600	8.95%	>	$421,900
Virginia	5.75%	>	$17,000	5.75%	>	$17,000
Washington	No State Income Tax			No State Income Tax		
West Virginia	6.50%	>	$60,000	6.50%	>	$60,000
Wisconsin	6.27%	>	$22,230	6.27%	>	$29,640
	7.65%	>	$244,750	7.65%	>	$326,330
Wyoming	No State Income Tax			No State Income Tax		
District of Columbia	8.50%	>	$60,000	8.50%	>	$60,000
	8.75%	>	$350,000	8.75%	>	$350,000
	8.95%	>	$1,000,000	8.95%	>	$1,000,000

Nicole Kaeding, "State Individual Income Tax Rates and Brackets for 2016," Tax Foundation, February 8, 2016, accessed June 23, 2016, http://taxfoundation.org/article/state-individual-income-tax-rates-and-brackets-2016.

Mike Sudermann, *The Executive Leap*, and its affiliates do not provide tax, legal or accounting advice. This material has been prepared for informational purposes only, and is not intended to provide, and should not be relied on for tax, legal or accounting advice.

Strategic Advising Services

How are you going to make *your* Executive Leap? Learn about the following tools to help you make the leap at www.theexecutiveleap.com:

- resume revamping
- executive leap toolkit
- LinkedIn workbook
- scripts to answer trap interview questions

- 1:1 interview strategies
- 1:1 strategic-advisor program
- webinars

MAKING THE EXECUTIVE LEAP?

Some of Mike's strategic-advisor clients include the following:

- CEO
- CFO
- CPO
- COO
- Senior VP
- VP

- Senior Director
- Director
- General Counsel
- Senior Manager
- And many more

HIRING?

Are you hiring and tired of lackluster results from HR or a lousy recruiter?

Enjoy flat fees, double placement guarantee, candidates in ten days or less, 100 percent acceptance rate, and five hundred locations across thirty countries?

Call Mike Sudermann, managing partner and executive recruiter for ASCENT Select Talent Capital, at 336-904-2329, or visit www.ascentselect.com.

Mike and his team work domestically and internationally within all industries on mid- and senior-level roles within supply chain, distribution, logistics, finance, operations, legal, and IT.

SAMPLING OF MIKE'S CLIENTS

- Bain & Co.
- Centerbridge Partners
- The Men's Wearhouse
- Crystal Creameries
- Billabong
- Ascena Retail Group
- Central Moloney
- Global Brands Group
- Cycle Gear
- Li & Fung, Ltd
- Frye Boots
- Burlington Coat Factory
- Sundial Brands
- Beacon Health Options
- Shoreline Construction
- Wynit Distribution
- Bond Mfg.

Printed in the USA
CPSIA information can be obtained
at www.ICGtesting.com
JSHW012029140824
68134JS00033B/2955